on track ...
Elton John

every album, every song
1969-1979

Peter Kearns

sonicbondpublishing.com

Sonicbond Publishing Limited
www.sonicbondpublishing.co.uk
Email: info@sonicbondpublishing.co.uk

First Published in the United Kingdom 2019
First Published in the United States 2019

British Library Cataloguing in Publication Data:
A Catalogue record for this book is available from the British Library

Copyright Peter Kearns 2019

ISBN 978-1-78952-034-7

Typset in ITC Garamond & Berthold Akzidenz Grotesk
Printed and bound in England

Graphic design and typesetting: Full Moon Media

on track ...
Elton John

Contents

With thanks to

Neil Barrett, Stephen Lambe and Kenny Passarell.

Would you like to write for Sonicbond Publishing?

At Sonicbond Publishing we are always on the look-out for authors, particularly for our two main series:

On Track. Mixing fact with in depth analysis, the On Track series examines the work of a particular musical artist or group. All genres are considered from easy listening and jazz to 60s soul to 90s pop, via rock and metal.

On Screen. This series looks at the world of film and television. Subjects considered include directors, actors and writers, as well as entire television and film series. As with the On Track series, we balance fact with analysis.

While professional writing experience would, of course, be an advantage the most important qualification is to have real enthusiasm and knowledge of your subject. First-time authors are welcomed, but the ability to write well in English is essential.

Sonicbond Publishing has distribution throughout Europe and North America, and all books are also published in E-book form. Authors will be paid a royalty based on sales of their book.

Further details are available from www.sonicbondpublishing.co.uk. To contact us, complete the contact form there or email info@sonicbondpublishing.co.uk

Introduction

The 1960s' culture revolution provided the colourful kaleidoscope that was the seed that spawned the music of Elton John. The unexpected losses of Marilyn Monroe and President John F. Kennedy led to the positive counteraction of The Beatles' debut American TV appearance on The Ed Sullivan Show in 1964 and the subsequent hold the band held over a developing generation. Inversely, the progressive flowering of the Summer of Love, leading to the gathering of the Woodstock Nation, was subsequently marred by negative social upheaval planting disillusion in the public psyche, subjugated by the finality of The Beatles' breakup in 1970. This was the collective precipice from which Elton John stepped into a pop culture in freefall.

Pop music now needed something new, if not to replace The Beatles, then to surpass them, as if such a thing could have been possible. Pop needed anything to keep the bar at its current height in an age when music and movies were the leading forms of entertainment, and the public knew the difference between the bogus and the genuine - a tall order, to put it mildly. As it happened, The Beatles *were* replaced, by an entirely new industry culture that they themselves had innovated and which became dominated by a handful of icons, of which Elton John became one.

Paul McCartney announced his departure from The Beatles on Friday 10 April 1970, the very day the *Elton John* album was first released. This UK issue contained the single 'Your Song' which would help break down doors for Elton in America. But getting to that point was no easy road.

Born Reginald Kenneth Dwight on 25 March 1947, his musical activity began in earnest with a five-year scholarship to London's Royal Academy of Music at the age of eleven. A job as an assistant at Mills Music followed, on weekends playing covers at the Northwood Hills Hotel near his home in Pinner Road, Harrow, in the Middlesex County of southeast England.

As a pianist, Reg formed the band Bluesology in 1962, which led to a number of professional touring engagements as backing band for visiting American soul artists such as Major Lance, the Isley Brothers, Lee Dorsey and Patti LaBelle.

Bluesology recorded two singles on the Fontana label under producer Jack Baverstock, who preferred Reg's voice to that of lead vocalist Stu Brown, resulting in the A-sides 'Come Back Baby' (1965) and 'Mr Frantic' (1966), both penned by Reg. They were the first of his songs to be committed to disc.

By September 1966, the band, now with a changed line-up, were regularly backing British blues singer Long John Baldry. The engagements continued, including Sunday 11 December 1966 which found the band doing a four-song session at The Beatles' recording home and now hallowed ground of EMI Studios on Abbey Road in St John's Wood, backing American R&B superstar Little Richard.

Feeling confined within the group and wishing to stretch out musically, Reg eventually departed, but not before answering a 'songwriters wanted' ad placed by Liberty Records in the *New Musical Express*. This led to him being paired with young Lincolnshire lyricist Bernie Taupin, who had answered the same ad. Liberty executive Ray Williams sent the two over to The Hollies' publishing company Gralto, which was administered by Dick James Music. Leaving Bluesology in late 1967, taking the names of saxophonist Elton Dean and singer John Baldry with him, the newly-named Elton John teamed up with Bernie officially, the two becoming staff songwriters for Dick James Records.

An Elton John solo album helmed by guitarist Caleb Quaye was recorded in 1968 and titled *Regimental Sgt Zippo*. It was a slightly uneven but not unrespectable set of sometimes lavishly orchestrated, psychedelic pop gems peppered with darker folk-like ballads. But under pressure from Dick James for more commercial material, Elton wrote and recorded 'I've Been Loving You', which became his first single. Credited to John/Taupin, it was produced by Caleb Quaye at Dick James Studios and released on Philips Records on Friday 1 March 1968.

Some of the *Regimental Sgt Zippo* material had been written with a view to being placed with other artists, but when publisher Steve Brown came on the scene to work for Dick James, he recommended that Elton and Bernie start writing for themselves. So, on the verge of pressing, the album was abandoned. Very quickly the two composers came up with 'Lady Samantha' and 'Skyline Pigeon', after which Steve Brown produced the 'Lady Samantha' single - Elton's second, but first to bear the writing credit John/Taupin.

Any book about Elton John's music also essentially covers Bernie Taupin's lyrics. The disciplines of the two are intertwined throughout the majority of the time period covered here, but lyrical analysis will appear only as necessary for enhancement. Album artwork will be touched on less, deserving as it is in the cases of *Goodbye Yellow Brick Road* and *Captain Fantastic and the Brown Dirt Cowboy* alone, of lengthy essay that is beyond the scope of this book.

All singles prior to the debut 1969 album *Empty Sky* will be covered, including those of Bluesology. The sections for the *17-11-70* and *Here and There* live albums will cover the complete track-listings according to their reissues - in the case of the former, the entire concert.

Some cover versions contemporary to the time of Elton's recordings of same will also be discussed. General commentary will focus on the songs and recordings with the occasional dive down a rabbit hole to more closely examine historic or technical audio aspects for added enhancement.

This book is intended to be a semi-critical exploration of an eclectic and original discography - unique music that sometimes appeared as out of step with its decade but ultimately helped to define it.

Early singles

Two Bluesology A-sides are worthy of mention as a lead-in to Elton's early singles proper. With both music and lyrics credited to Reg Dwight, 'Come Back Baby' (1965) and 'Mr Frantic' (1966) had blues standards sung by Stu Brown as B-sides. A new Bluesology line-up followed the B-side formula for both sides of the third single 'Since I Found You Baby' released on Polydor in October 1967, after which Reg left the group.

'Come Back Baby' (Reg Dwight)

Released as a single A-side, July 1965 (UK), b/w 'Times Getting Tougher Than Tough'.

The first of three Bluesology singles, 'Come Back Baby' written by Reg was a middle-of-the-road outing in the cabaret style. You can imagine him walking around the tables, microphone in hand, pleading to anyone willing to look up from their steak and chips. Elton has since expressed displeasure with it, but pleasing chordal moves were present, as was that singular singing-voice, already displaying an individual character. The recording was produced by Jack Baverstock on Thursday 3 June 1965 at Philips Studios, London.

'Mr Frantic' (Reg Dwight)

Released as a single A-side, February 1966 (UK), b/w 'Every Day (I Have the Blues)'.

Recorded on Thursday 18 November 1965 and released on Fontana Records, the second Bluesology single saw Reg return to lead vocal duties. His delivery hallmarks were again audible, but success for the song was not to be, possibly due to the title being difficult to understand when heard on the recording. This was a shame when the piece was stylistically more in line with contemporary pop than the first single.

'I've Been Loving You' (Elton John)

Released as a single A-side, 1 March 1968 (UK), b/w 'Here's to the Next Time'.

Produced by Caleb Quaye at Dick James Studios in December 1967, Elton's first solo single showed the development of a more professional sound. The performances were tight, the vocal confident, and a shrill string section sweetened proceedings. But the composition, credited to John/Taupin but, in fact, completely Elton's work, was hindered by a confused lyric.

With Elton and Bernie being under pressure from Dick James, the song was an effort to sound commercial and was not typical of the material Elton was recording. So in light of that fact, the track was, if not commercially successful, an artistic triumph if that's quantifiable by whether it achieves its original objective.

Elton's songs of the time certainly attracted cover versions and 'I've Been Loving You' was no exception. Hot on the heels of the single came a complimentary if less-inspiring version by Edwin Bee, released on Decca Records in May 1968.

'Here's to the Next Time' (Elton John)
Released as a single B-side, July 1965 (UK), b/w 'I've Been Loving You'.
Accented by an impressive horn section, this blues-based B-side comes across
now as more accomplished and adventurous than its above companion.
Lyrically it shared a similar theme to the A-side if more resigned than hopeful.
No chart position was achieved for the single, but the potential was plain to
hear.

'The Angel Tree' (Elton John, Bernie Taupin)
Released as a single B-side, 1 March 1968 (Portugal), b/w 'I've Been Loving You'.
'I've Been Loving You' was later issued as a four-song EP in Portugal, making
'The Angel Tree' the first officially released John/Taupin composition. This
recording was extracted from the ill-fated Regimental Sgt Zippo album of
1968. The lyric alluded to the legend of a tree Bernie used to visit as a child
in Lincolnshire. The tale claimed that an angel living within the tree visited a
shepherd sitting beneath it, the angel claiming to have an important message
for mankind from God. Taking the message to the village, the shepherd was
stoned and cast out as a madman, eventually dying in poverty with the message
left untold.
   The recording has a sprightly, bubblegum pop approach with a 'la-la' refrain
punctuated by a tight horn section. The title was later referenced in Taupin's
'Burn Down the Mission' opening line, 'You tell me there's an angel in your
tree'.

'Thank You for All of Your Loving' (Elton John, Caleb Quaye)
Released as a single B-side, 1 March 1968 (Portugal), b/w 'I've Been Loving You'.
Accompanying 'The Angel Tree' on the four-song Portugal EP was this lively
funk/soul jam made as a demo for the UK band, Dukes Noblemen. Their
version, featuring Elton on piano, was issued as a B-side on Philips Records in
July 1968. It was the first released co-write by Elton and guitarist Caleb Quaye,

'Lady Samantha' (Elton John, Bernie Taupin)
Released as a single A-side, 17 January 1969 (UK), January 1970 (US), b/w 'All
Across the Havens'.
Produced by Steve Brown near the beginning of the *Empty Sky* sessions in
December 1968, this witchy second single was the first of Elton's A-sides with a
Bernie lyric. It had the mythical flavour that coloured much of Bernie's output
at the time. The players were the rhythm section for *Empty Sky* - Roger Pope:
drums, Tony Murray: bass, and Caleb Quaye: guitar.
   Failing to chart, it did receive generous airplay in the UK, becoming a
turntable hit. It made little impression in the USA until covered by American
rock band Three Dog Night for their 1969 album *Suitable for Framing*, which
went gold in the USA later that year, providing Elton with a tangible leg-up into
the American market.

'All Across the Havens' (Elton John, Bernie Taupin)

Released as a single B-side, 17 January 1969 (UK), January 1970 (US), b/w 'Lady Samantha'.

Like its A-side 'Lady Samantha', this folk-rock B-side had an esoteric lyric. Lines like 'The water withdrew, leaving me standing on a road leading through' possessed a lucid imagery worthy of any contemporary Taupin work. In its down-home but hip treatment, it appeared to owe a debt to The Band, sounding more American than any Elton track to this point. Not only did this song supply a semi-conceptual style template of sorts for the future *Tumbleweed Connection* album, but it also set a standard for the increasingly outstanding B-sides that were to follow.

'It's Me That You Need' (Elton John, Bernie Taupin)

Released as a single A-side, 16 May 1969 (UK), b/w 'Just Like Strange Rain'.

The follow-up single to 'Lady Samantha' was recorded near the end of the *Empty Sky* sessions and was the moment Elton's voice began sounding like the guy on the big hits to come. His style was coming into its own and here for the first time were signature vocal interjections that became familiar aural identifiers throughout the '70s.

Musically the introduction pre-empted the feel of 'I Need You to Turn To' from the *Elton John* album, but the progressing verse gave way to more dramatic flair with its biting celli hinting toward 'Take Me to the Pilot'. However, today the flute-laden mood sounds dated, even for 1969, working at odds with the grit of Caleb's guitar, so you get the feeling that the arrangement didn't quite know what it wanted to be.

Not as instantly accessible as the comparatively self-explanatory 'Lady Samantha', this new semi-esoteric single might have made more sense if released after *Empty Sky*, instead of three weeks prior. This might have made it a sufficient stepping stone to the stirring follow-up single 'Border Song' and its accompanying album, *Elton John*.

'Just Like Strange Rain' (Elton John, Bernie Taupin)

Released as a single B-side, 16 May 1969 (UK), b/w 'It's Me That You Need'.

The musical composition and production treatment of this B-side did not match the colourful and engaging lyric. Both the depth beneath and the psychedelic surface atop its 21 scant lines appeared neglected by an overly-simple chord progression dressed in a carefree, almost bubblegum pop costume, barely distinguished by a semi-interesting key-change into the chorus. A bass guitar cue successfully conquered earlier in the song was fumbled at 2m:24s. Though not a dud note per se, an evident pitch issue facilitated the flub, highlighting what can only be construed as the intentional filling of the B-side with whatever material was at hand.

But this was April 1969, late in the game for psychedelia. You can easily imagine Elton recognising the lyrical value, clocking the approaching use-by date of the psychedelic trend and choosing to decorate the track minimally. Perhaps thrown on the backburner at first, it certainly deserved resurrection, at least to B-side status.

Empty Sky (1969)

Personnel:
Elton John: vocals, keyboards
Tony Murray: bass
Roger Pope, Nigel Olsson: drums
Caleb Quaye: guitars
Graham Vickery: harmonica
Roger Pope, Caleb Quaye: percussion
Don Fay: saxophone, flute
Clive Franks: whistling
Recorded: December 1968-April 1969 at Dick James Studios, London
Producer: Steve Brown
Engineer: Frank Owen
Release date: 3 June 1969 (UK), 13 Jan. 1975 (US)
Chart placings: UK: did not chart, US: 6.

Elton's debut album proper was recorded with him in a central position to producer Steve Brown on one side encouraging John and Taupin to write what they please, and publishing colossus Dick James on the other calling for commercial material. This was a predicament that many newly-forming pop stars could only dream of being tormented by.

The result was music eclectic in style but with unification coming from all involved, believing they were on to something. At the time, Elton described *Empty Sky* as 'The greatest thing I'd ever heard'. Despite psychedelia's approaching dissolve, Bernie continued with his colourful and ambiguous style, the album offering up work that was for both writers their finest example to date.

Reviews were positive. Cashbox's Eric Lustbader was moved to do a write-up on Elton regardless of the lack of an American release. It appeared in US record stores in January 1975 when it was issued with cover art by Belgian artist Jean Michel Folon replacing the original art by David Larkham. The album then reached number 6 on the *Billboard* Pop Album chart.

'Empty Sky' (Elton John, Bernie Taupin)

Released as a single B-side, 1971 (France), b/w 'Love Song'.
The title-track opener, composed to Bernie's lyric on Tuesday 7 January 1969, gave the album an almost avant-garde jazz-inspired introduction with its rhythmic conga pattern - a nod to the Rolling Stones' 'Sympathy for The Devil'. This was punctuated by piano accents confident enough to include a seemingly purposeful bum-note repetition fuelled more by humour than pretence. The accents eventually gave way to the full band and an immediately urgent vocal that matched the desperation of the lyric and its incarcerated protagonist.

The close of the second chorus brought the eerily gorgeous backwards guitar solo that mirrored The Beatles' similar 'I'm Only Sleeping' technique. The soothing bridge leads to the introduction of a love interest in the following verse, despite the narrator's paranoia that 'Sooner or later you'll own just one half of this land, By shining your eyes on the wealth of every man'. It's a narrative depth that was appearing increasingly in pop lyrics. These ingredients contributed to a rock-solid and intriguing eight-and-a-half-minute journey more than worthy of the three-minute single edit it was granted in 1971 in France, albeit as B-side to 'Love Song'.

The recording concluded with a slice of sonic innovation. A successful attempt was made to create a macro-dynamic in the performance where there was none naturally committed to tape. Towards the end when Elton sings 'I want you to shoosh', the band is faded down and some soft piano overdubbed in the gap to create the effect of the musicians doing as he says. Chic phrases like 'Get down with it baby' tarnished the affair to a point, but the overall effect was intact and not unlike the dynamics Elton's future band would create in live performances, such as those captured on the 1971 *17-11-70* album.

Dynamics aside, *Empty Sky*'s sole true rock track was dominated by a consistent and satisfying attitude that wouldn't be repeated to quite the same level until the single release of 'Saturday Night's Alright for Fighting' in June 1973. Though in 1969 Elton was unclear of future musical direction, patterns were nevertheless forming.

'Valhalla' (Elton John, Bernie Taupin)

Elton and Bernie soaked up their early influences like sponges, purging them almost imperceptibly into their work. Elton later described 'Valhalla' as being Leonard Cohen-esque.

Bernie's love of Norse mythology was close to the surface too. Valhalla was the place the God Odin chose to send half the souls who died in battle, the rest going to the goddess Freja. Odin appeared to be the narrator, but the mythical content was balanced by a certain level of emotional gravitas.

Instrumentally the piece featured harpsichord periodically interjecting above the band and a truly late-'60s-sounding Hammond organ. Innovation reappeared in the form of the band fading out leaving the harpsichord unaccompanied, striking a repetitive blues dominant 7th note in the home key on the fade-out. I refer to innovation in general, as experimentation was encouraged and recording artists were struggling to compete with the techniques of The Beatles whose every invented trick was aped and branded into the repertoire. But Elton and co kept tricks to a minimum, and they were bringing a fairly original sound to the table anyway.

'Western Ford Gateway' (Elton John, Bernie Taupin)

As a break from the stress of the first song and the intellect of the second, 'Western Ford Gateway' was a fairly standard folk-rock romp. But there was still plenty of room for lyrical interpretation. Jumping from past and present tense to straight reporting, the stanzas were brief but with clear imagery of cold streets and drunken tavern-dwellers. The melodically hooky chorus appropriately betrayed the lyrical abstraction just as any fine pop song should. But the song was merely a hint of future strengths, or even of those to come as the album progressed.

'Hymn 2000' (Elton John, Bernie Taupin)

Caleb Quaye's discordant acoustic guitar intruding on the introduction of the jaunty Pied Piper-like 'Hymn 2000', immediately grabs attention. (Pan to the left for clarity). The chords change key, moving restlessly through the verse before levelling out to a more conventional harmony for the chorus.

The abstract lyrics are fun but the wordplay is also gruesome with religious overtones. The line 'Collecting submarine numbers on the main street of the sea' hints at the Beatles, if not downright foreshadowing their yet-to-be-released 'Octopus's Garden', issued on Abbey Road three months after *Empty Sky*. A further foreshadowing occurs in the flute lines floating across the rich verse chords, a combination sounding uncannily like a future Genesis arrangement circa 1972. But the constant flute here becomes laborious, especially when joined in the chorus by the organ melodies on the opposite side of the stereo spectrum - the two vying for attention in ignorance of the vocal, causing a sense of information overload. However the rich lyrical imagery and nods to the progressive make 'Hymn 2000' interesting and the most bizarre *Empty Sky* track of them all.

'Lady, What's Tomorrow?' (Elton John, Bernie Taupin)

Taupin's well of subject matter was seemingly bottomless, this time moving into ecology mode. An older brother warns the younger of the unavoidable progression from natural beauty to concrete. Though she is the target of the title question, who the lady is, and how she fits in is kept a mystery.

The recording is fairly conventional if unremarkable, typical medium-tempo pop fare. But the track acts as a landmark on the journey, being the debut of drummer Nigel Olsson on an Elton John recording.

'Sails' (Elton John, Bernie Taupin)

Released as a single B-side, 1972 (NZ), b/w 'Levon'.

'Sails' puts us back in a rock mode, more direct but less edgy than the title track. Roger Pope and Tony Murray supply a tight and unshakable rhythm section here, complemented by Wurlitzer electric piano alongside Caleb's tasteful electric rhythm chunks. After the first chorus, the central section of the track opens out into a lengthy guitar solo.

Lyrically the location is a seaport, a place Bernie's lyrics would periodically return to. The narrator seeks the attention of Lucy, who blinds him literally with her hand across his eyes and figuratively with her guess of 'the number of bales in the back room'.

Bereft of the seriousness of earlier tracks, and perhaps the most likely potential single present, 'Sails' expresses a more carefree and accessible attitude. As if to reflect this, Elton and band performed this song and 'Lady Samantha' live on BBC Radio One on Monday 14 July 1969.

'The Scaffold' (Elton John, Bernie Taupin)

Impenetrable in its lyrical layering, 'The Scaffold' plumbed the depths of license, being more poem than lyric. Interpretation still seems virtually impossible beyond the suggestion of a scaffold being a place to head for to 'jump the gun'. Ironic maybe, but still too deep to secure anything approaching levity in this mysterious hodge-podge of mythical themes and narrative confession.

Lacking any fun or satisfactory level of explanation, 'The Scaffold' was carefully placed towards the end of proceedings, saved by the contrast of the following 'Skyline Pigeon'. In its defence, the performance approach is light-hearted and even flippant. As if to dismiss the lyrical weight altogether, the slow shuffle rhythm is light on its feet, tripping the light fantastic in defiance, allowing an engaging listen, if not a repeated one.

'Skyline Pigeon' (Elton John, Bernie Taupin)

Compared to earlier tracks, 'Skyline Pigeon' is startling enough in its contrast and accomplishment to be mistaken for a cover song. It could easily have been considered so by anyone familiar with the overwrought August 1968 Roger James Cooke version on Columbia Records, replete with lyric mistakes. Guy Darrell's denim-soaked jangle of a version on Pye that same month equally granted the song few favours. Judith Durham's 1970 cover at least gave the song an extra dimension, even if it was one of insanity with the manic speed at which she rushed through the choruses. That version hammered the point across in a most disturbing fashion indeed.

Gone were the mythical characters and ancient themes found elsewhere on *Empty Sky*, replaced with the possible metaphor of marriage-as-prison suggested by the line 'This aching metal ring', which tied the concept in nicely with the incarceration of the title track. Mysteriously, Guy Darrell chose the baffling lyrical substitute, 'This aching memory'.

Some have interpreted this lyric literally as the wish of a bird to be freed from its cage, which along with the marriage concept seems simplistic. Some room remains for interpretation. In a 1997 *Billboard* magazine interview, Bernie stated that he preferred people to draw their own conclusions and that it's much more fun if someone comes up with a theory of their own. Beneath the emotive vocal, sung out on the fire escape at DJM, the minimal instrumentation is harpsichord with the entry of additional organ at the second verse. This gives the piece a hymnal quality that begs the suggestion that the narrator is married not to a spouse, but to the church. He wants to hear the pealing bells of distant churches. This idea provides one possible opportunity to dive for pearls; the song seems so willing to yield to anyone willing to search hard enough. One mark of a well-written song is that it can offer new possibilities over time. Interpretation is not limited to words when music can equally provide clues. 'Skyline Pigeon' is no exception, given that it was considered as Elton and Bernie's first real head-turner.

'Gulliver/Hay-Chewed' (Elton John, Bernie Taupin)

The sentimental but resigned 'Gulliver' set the tone as the seed of many signature ballads that would grace Elton's repertoire from here on out. It paved the way for 'The King Must Die', 'My Father's Gun' and 'Burn Down the Mission'.

By resigned, I mean that this lurching lament to the death of a family dog never spills over into a tear-jerker. From the outset, John and Taupin demonstrated this skill that prevented their music from becoming overly saccharine - a borderline arguably uncrossed until the appearance of 'Sorry Seems to Be the Hardest Word' in 1976. The ending instrumental jazz jam 'Hay-Chewed' also avoids the possibility by leaving the listener no option but to smile. Unrelated but nevertheless a pun on The Beatles' 'Hey Jude', the jam leads directly into a sequential audio collage of the album's tracks, ending on a hard cut not unlike the end of The Beatles' 'I Want You (She's So Heavy)' from their *Abbey Road* - an album that *Empty Sky* was a contemporary of.

Elton John (1970)

Personnel:
Elton John: vocals, piano, harpsichord
Frank Clark: acoustic bass
Madeline Bell, Tony Burrows, Roger Cook, Lesley Duncan, Kay Garner, Tony Hazzard: backing vocals
Les Hurdle, Dave Richmond, Alan Weighill: bass
Paul Buckmaster: solo cello
Barbara Moore: choir lead
Terry Cox, Barry Morgan: drums
Frank Clark, Colin Green, Roland Harker, Clive Hicks, Alan Parker, Caleb Quaye: guitars
Skaila Kanga: Harp
Brian Dee: organ
Dennis Lopez, Tex Navarra: percussion
Diana Lewis: synthesizer
Recorded: Jan. 1970 at Trident Studios, London
Producer: Gus Dudgeon
Engineer: Robin Geoffrey Cable
Arranger: Paul Buckmaster
Release date: 10 April 1970 (UK), 22 July 1970 (US)
Chart placings: UK: 5, US: 4, CAN: 4, AUS: 4

Fresh from working with David Bowie, orchestral arranger Paul Buckmaster was hired to work on the *Elton John* album. Scoring had commenced when Beatles producer George Martin was invited to produce the record. Conflicting stories exist as to why this never eventuated. One says that Martin simply declined and the other that he agreed to on the condition that he also arrange the album. Elton turned this down preferring to remain with Buckmaster as arranger. His work on the *Elton John* album ultimately encapsulated not only orchestral arrangement but also parts for guitar, bass and drums, 'No Shoestrings On Louise' being an example of this.

Through Buckmaster came producer Gus Dudgeon. Elton later described the recording process as being 'Like an army manoeuvre with Gus as Sgt. Major.' The project was certainly a step-up from *Empty Sky*, with recording taking place at London's Trident Studios and an army of session players enlisted to highlight selected tracks. 'Your Song' alone had three guitarists, not to mention half the tracks including an orchestra, which Elton played with live. Taking into account a picturesque and exotic development in Bernie's lyrics, the combined audio effect of all as a development from *Empty Sky* to here, was analogous to the visual advancement from Super 8 to Cinemascope.

'Your Song' (Elton John, Bernie Taupin)

Released as a single A-side, 7 January 1971 (UK), b/w 'Into the Old Man's Shoes'.

UK: 7. AUS: 11. NZ: 18.

Released as a single B-side, 26 October 1970 (US), b/w 'Take Me to the Pilot'. US: 8 CAN: 3.

On Monday 27 October 1969, Elton composed 'Your Song' from Bernie's lyric. His recording was preceded by Three Dog Night's cover on their *It Ain't Easy* album in March 1970. Elton's recording was dressed in the prevalent easy-listening pop ballad style and placed as album-opener – a clever way to seduce the listener and sneak-through the upcoming dramatic oeuvre that was to sprout from the song's ear-pleasing but conventional seed.

Before becoming a ubiquitous hit, 'Your Song' was issued as the B-side of 'Take Me to the Pilot' in the USA where it became the preferred choice for airplay.

Lyrically the song is more than a mere innocent expression of romantic admiration. The second verse refers almost entirely to the act of writing the lyric itself, which led to the myth that it was written on the roof at Dick James Music. The truth is less glamorous, Bernie having simply dashed it out over breakfast at Elton's home in 1969. The words securely insulate themselves against possible criticism by admitting their ineptitude for the task at hand, finally fumbling across the complimentary finish line. Clever stuff, and it all rolls off Elton's tongue as smooth as silk without suggesting a hint of self-indulgence. Art and commerce hand in hand, and possibly Elton's finest example of that particular phenomenon.

On the surface, 'Your Song' was subtle, a creeper if you like, compared to contemporary masterpieces like Simon & Garfunkel's 'Bridge Over Troubled Water' or The Beatles' 'The Long and Winding Road'. But it fulfilled its function perfectly, pinpointing a specific generic co-ordinate to which Elton and Bernie need not necessarily return.

'I Need You to Turn To' (Elton John, Bernie Taupin)

Track two enters slightly uneasy territory. The atmosphere of harpsichord, nylon-stringed acoustic guitar and string section keeps the tone mellow, so you know you're in a similar neighbourhood to 'Your Song' but minus a rhythm section as a guide. The clear river of that song flows into this saltwater which has a calm surface but is deeper and darker. The narrator's admiration is desperate, and he admits to losing control, an un-nerving weakness that can only be subdued by the availability of the second person.

'I Need You to Turn To' is a brief taste of the drama that gives the album life further down the groove. It's a singular saline drip, gone in a flash so as not to unsettle you too much.

'Take Me to the Pilot' (Elton John, Bernie Taupin)

Released as a single A-side, 26 October 1970 (US and CAN), b/w 'Your Song'.

The perfect foil for what came before it, 'Take Me to the Pilot' brought some welcome rock and roll relief with Caleb Quaye's chunky rhythm guitar style to

17

the fore. New to the fray, Paul Buckmaster and his angry celli took a stylistic cue to develop on from 'It's Me That You Need'.

Gone were the sugar and salt of the first two songs, replaced by a lyrical flavour cryptic enough to be immune from assessment. If David Bowie had recorded an Elton John cover in 1970, this would have been the perfect choice. Abstract in approach and edgy in declaration, it could believably be a conceptual lyric template of sorts for parts of Bowie's *The Man Who Sold the World*, which came later in the year.

Title identification notwithstanding, 'Take Me to the Pilot' shared in the chart success of 'Your Song', its original flipside outside the UK.

'No Shoestrings on Louise' (Elton John, Bernie Taupin)

Intended as a Rolling Stones send-up, this country waltz arranged from top to bottom by Paul Buckmaster, harked toward the Americana themes of *Tumbleweed Connection* and represented a development in Elton's singing. The twang he adopted in jest here was destined to subtly reappear as the ideal companion to Bernie's coming odes to America's west and south. The naturally flowing vocal technique was never overstated and even occasionally crept into later material for which it was likely unintended.

This song also introduced a dark lyrical exoticism that established an ongoing undercurrent in the subsoil of Bernie's conceptual repertoire. This was timely. The sexual revolution had happened, so that topic was freely approachable, which merely provided a license for additional taboo motifs to spice things up sporadically. This development crept into the lyrics over time with the reaction of a match to petroleum in slow motion.

'First Episode at Hienton' (Elton John, Bernie Taupin)

Every song on the *Elton John* album was a musical statement in itself, so it made perfect sense when producer Gus Dudgeon later stated that the album was initially conceived as an elaborate demo of Elton's songs with the intention of getting them placed with other artists.

Startling in its compositional maturity, 'First Episode at Hienton' turned yet another corner, revealing more surprises. Its vivid recollection of young love gave a sense of watching an old home movie. The strings here were the first powerful exposure of arranger Paul Buckmaster on an Elton record. Subtle and understated compared to coming orchestral intensities, there was nevertheless an undercurrent of unfinished business built into this arrangement.

By the word 'arrangement', I refer not only to the string section but the instrumentation as a whole, which was masterfully manipulated to communicate the ideas. It's still a fascinating listen today. The general mood is gloom, as emphasised by the raining low string lines, but with shafts of sunlight occasionally filtering through. The eerie Moog synthesizer compliments of Diana Lewis creeps around the middle bridge section giving the track a sudden modern makeover, as does Caleb Quaye's trembling tremolo guitar toward the closing section. Highlighting specific moments, all these details not only create tension but keep the listener focused on the unfolding reminiscence to the end.

Astonishingly, in this period, Elton didn't write his songs down, preferring to store them in his head. It's unthinkable that a milestone such as this song could have been lost in a flash, as fast as he and Bernie were making them appear.

'Sixty Years On' (Elton John, Bernie Taupin)

The initial release of 'Sixty Years On' was as a fascinating cover along with two other Elton songs on San Francisco rock band Silver Metre's self-titled 1969 album. Without Elton's recorded version as a guide, the band took the song to an utterly British sound, not unlike that of progressive group Rare Bird. The recording also stylistically pre-empted the Genesis live staple 'The Knife' by at least a year.

Did Elton influence progressive rock? Doubtful, but Paul Buckmaster's orchestral arrangements were futuristic and formidable, to say the least, and never so much, at least to this point, as on Elton's recorded version of this simple hymn-made-huge. The internal framework of this dramatic piece acts as a photographic negative to that of 'First Episode at Hienton'. Where that song was lyrically substantial but kept instrumentally simple, this one was aurally expansive and its poetry minimal.

A touching tribute to Bernie's grandfather, the mood was generally kept light with nylon-stringed acoustic guitar and not a piano in sight. The orchestra, however, slightly over-compensates for the poignant lyrics. Listening today, the entire concoction is still inescapably captivating with its buzzing Ligeti-esque string lines, blatantly unrelated and exotic eastern cello motif leading into the vocal, and pounding Stravinskian rhythmic accents, all in a sense bemoaning the onset of ageing as if it were avoidable. But it's a hell of a listening experience. After all, where pop songs necessarily compress a bigger idea down to its essentials, who's to say Elton and co couldn't take the literary approach of taking a humble idea and making it massive?

'Border Song' (Elton John, Bernie Taupin)

Released as a single A-side, 20 March 1970 (UK), 24 April 1970 (US), b/w 'Bad Side of the Moon'. US: 92. CAN: 34.

Issued as a single almost a month prior to the *Elton John* album in the UK but failing to make an impact there, 'Border Song' fared better in Canada where it was Elton's debut singles chart appearance anywhere, entering the chart on 8 August. Peaking at 92 in the USA, it was trounced later in the year by Aretha Franklin's more popular cover version achieving number 37.

A cry of alienation, but dressed in gospel clothes, the song's lack of evangelism rendered it more of a gospel-blues piece turned on its head by Elton's pleading lyric contribution of the final verse. At that point the concept suddenly focused into view, expressing an ideal which gave the song a topical relevance.

Like 'No Shoestrings on Louise' before it, 'Border Song' gave a hint towards the outright Americana that would find its full flowering on *Tumbleweed Connection*.

'The Greatest Discovery' (Elton John, Bernie Taupin)

This deceptively simple family snapshot is a triumph of lyrical focus meeting complimentary melody, worthy of Rodgers and Hammerstein. It is side two's central moment of tranquillity, overshadowed by the comparatively towering behemoths of 'Sixty Years On' and 'The King Must Die'.

'The Cage' (Elton John, Bernie Taupin)

'The Cage' signals the re-emergence of the newfound exotic vein that set the lyrics alight in 'No Shoestrings on Louise'. The psychologically untouchable antagonist spits his vitriol carelessly - a mode that when coupled with Diana Lewis' creepy synth clusters, creates a formula that would not be misplaced on the *Goodbye Yellow Brick Road* album.

The snarling horn section recalls The Beatles' 'Savoy Truffle' and predicts Elton's own 'You're So Static'. This gives 'The Cage' an edge, helping it fulfil a similar function to 'Take Me to the Pilot' on side one - that is, some rock to shake off the stresses of the encapsulating ballad epics.

'The King Must Die' (Elton John, Bernie Taupin)

In the sequence of the album, the peak of orchestral dynamics had passed with 'Sixty Years On', taking the heat off 'The King Must Die'. As a result, the song progressed naturally allowing Elton's voice to carry the momentum. Orchestral peaks were understated, the strings more active making tasteful interjections in the central section.

This exploration of how the mighty can fall from their pedestals reached its climax with Elton performing one of the most powerful and acrobatic vocal lines of his career, leading to the final line, 'Long live the king'. A fitting end to the story, crowned with a clever musical touch, where with the exception of Elton's piano the musicians land on the root chord minus the third, suggesting an ultimately hollow victory.

Contemporary Tracks:
'Bad Side of the Moon' (Elton John, Bernie Taupin)

Released as a single B-side, 20 March 1970 (UK), 24 April 1970 (US), b/w 'Border Song'.

This science-fiction-inspired song found its first release as a single by UK group Toe Fat in February 1970. Heavier than Elton's version, it headed in a more progressive rock direction and even borrowed the riff from Led Zeppelin's

'Whole Lotta Love'.

Elton's rendering was more laid-back but still had vigorous energy thanks to strong production. The orchestral arrangement displayed some of arranger Paul Buckmaster's forming signature moves which became synonymous with Elton John's work. The track eventually found album release on the rarities collection, *Lady Samantha*, issued first on cassette in 1974 and then on vinyl in 1980.

Rock band April Wine had a Top 20 hit in Canada with a livelier version of the song in 1972.

'From Denver to L.A.' (Francis Lai, Hal Shaper)

Released as a single A-side, May 1970 (US), b/w 'Warm Summer Rain'.

Featured in British sports movie *The Games*, this MOR love song sung by Elton was a cover released as a single in the USA on Viking Records. It was nicely orchestrated and produced by Christian Gaubert at Olympic Studios, London, in 1969, with a B-side performed by the Barbara Moore Singers. But its release was viewed as a cash-in on Elton's newfound success, and an injunction was swiftly put on it, stopping it in its tracks.

'Rock and Roll Madonna' (Elton John, Bernie Taupin)

Released as a single A-side, 19 June 1970 (UK), b/w 'Grey Seal'.

A mysterious choice for a freestanding single, this simple rock and roll dirge was issued in the UK, Europe and New Zealand, causing not a ripple. It may have been an attempt at some UK singles chart presence after 'Border Song' failed to make a mark there.

The recording is notable in that it features Deep Purple bassist, Roger Glover, and brings back *Empty Sky* drummer Roger Pope.

'Grey Seal' (Elton John, Bernie Taupin)

Released as a single B-side, 19 June 1970 (UK), b/w 'Rock and Roll Madonna'.

Bernie Taupin has always claimed this lyric was nothing but meaningless imagery. Elton describes it as being like a Dali painting. It's certainly rich with interpretation potential, and though this early version lacked the defining veracity of that recorded a few years later for *Goodbye Yellow Brick Road*, it made up for it by being another Paul Buckmaster arranging triumph.

Oddly lounge-esque with the inclusion of vibraphone, the chorus balances that feeling with the textural counterpoint of individual synthesizer lines, giving the recording a modern flavour for its time. Also unique to this version is the psychedelic string arrangement which rides the coda out in a grand and dispassionate manner.

'Into the Old Man's Shoes' (Elton John, Bernie Taupin)

Released as a single B-side, 7 January 1971 (UK), b/w 'Your Song'.

This leftover from the *Elton John* sessions was also passed over for

Tumbleweed Connection. By naming the Arizona town of Tombstone, the lyric hinted at the coming Americana which would pervade Bernie's output for a time. This is perhaps what qualified it as more suitable for inclusion on the 2008 *Tumbleweed* extended re-issue.

The lyric shows the narrator to be quite paranoid upon his father's death, giving the song an air of dark self-indulgence with little if any sign of hope. But the recording is historically interesting when considered as a stepping-stone from the forlorn orchestration of *Elton John* to the politically-informed swamp-funk coming.

Tumbleweed Connection (1970)

Personnel:
Elton John: vocals, piano, Hammond organ
Leslie Duncan, Mike Egan, Caleb Quaye, Les Thatcher: acoustic guitar
Madeline Bell, Tony Burrows, Lesley Duncan, Kay Garner, Tony Hazzard, Tammi
Hunt, Dee Murray, Nigel Olsson, Dusty Springfield, Sue and Sunny, Heather
Wheatman, Yvonne Wheatman: backing vocals
Herbie Flowers, Dave Glover, Dee Murray: bass
Chris Laurence: double bass
Barry Morgan, Nigel Olsson, Roger Pope: drums
Caleb Quaye: electric guitar
Ian Duck: harmonica
Skaila Kanga: Harp
Karl Jenkins: oboe
Brian Dee: organ
Robin Jones, Roger Pope: percussion
Gordon Huntley: steel guitar
Johnny Van Derek: violin
Recorded: March 1970 at Trident Studios, London
Producer: Gus Dudgeon
Engineer: Robin Geoffrey Cable
Arranger: Paul Buckmaster
Release date: 30 October 1970 (UK), 4 January 1971 (US)
Chart placings: UK: 2, US: 5, CAN: 4, AUS: 4

For half of *Tumbleweed Connection*, guitarist, Caleb Quaye, enlisted his fellow
Hookfoot band members. Drummer Roger Pope had played on most of *Empty
Sky,* and now bassist Dave Glover came into the fold. All were DJM session
players. The group gave a consistency to 'Ballad of a Well-Known Gun', 'Son of
Your Father', 'My Father's Gun' and 'Where To Now St Peter?'. Hookfoot singer
Ian Duck even contributed harmonica to 'Country Comfort' and 'Son of Your
Father'.

The album had a more straight-ahead band sound than *Elton John,*
providing an accessible base to carry the stealthy topics which ranged from
industrialisation and vigilantism to religion and war in tales taking place in the
American west and south. A rough style indicator could be swamp rock as the
material was certainly informed by American group The Band, and specifically
their 1968 masterpiece *Music from Big Pink*. In turn, *Tumbleweed* itself has
been suggested as an influence on American country rock bands such as Lynyrd
Skynyrd and Eagles. True or not, *Tumbleweed Connection* was a fine tribute to
Americana, if criticised in some quarters for lack of lyrical attention to detail.
Regardless, due to its style and subject matter, it was praiseworthy, widely
noted as being so even more for the fact that these recordings were made prior
to Elton or Bernie ever visiting the USA.

'Ballad of a Well-Known Gun' (Elton John, Bernie Taupin)

The opening of *Tumbleweed Connection* was a stylistic contrast to *Elton John* – just as accessible but in a different way. Where 'Your Song' was a radio-friendly pop gem, 'Ballad of a Well-Known Gun' was a deeper cut that immediately sucked you into its world with a clever intro trick where the rhythm appeared to miss a beat (it simply began on beat 4 of a 4/8 bar). With the rhythm track recorded in one take, producer Gus Dudgeon requested that Caleb Quaye overdub the initial chickin'-pickin' guitar that brings in the piano and drums, allowing the strands of music to gain momentum rolling into one another, much like a tumbleweed.

These guys were getting good at this record-making lark now, becoming experts in balancing intellectual content with commercial cues, and slick instrumentation with irresistible hooks. Whether aware of it or not, they knew the formula for satisfying both the casual and hardcore listener along the journey of an album so that the initiate kept listening and the convert remained interested.

The track bore a stylistic similarity to The Band, whose 1968 roots-rock Americana masterpiece, *Music from Big Pink*, had spawned a small coterie of sound-alike efforts. But no one adopted the concept in quite the same way Elton and band did. 'Ballad of a Well-Known Gun' was funkier than The Band's more collectively liquid approach to arrangement, and *Tumbleweed*'s overall sound was distinctly brighter and in-your-face, allowing individual instrumental parts to jump out for attention.

Originally recorded at London's Olympic Studio circa September/October 1969 in a more twee up-tempo country style, 'Ballad of a Well-Known Gun', the story of an 1800s fugitive on the run and caught by the Pinkertons, came to its cinematic fore in the half-time swamp groove it entrenched in the landscape here.

Popular with musicians, the song was covered first by Silver Metre in 1969, in a shallow take featuring myriad lyrical mistakes too numerous to mention. In 1971, Kate Taylor, sister of American folk-pop troubadour, James Taylor, released a fine version that moved between double and half-time. Shortly thereafter, came an overly-emoted version by the band Pollution that rendered the lyric as unconvincing.

Elton's recording won the day with its many strengths, which included the added bonus of Dusty Springfield in the backing vocal group. But the lion's share of the credit must surely go to the rhythm track and its interplay between Elton, Caleb, drummer Roger Pope and bassist Dave Glover, providing perhaps the finest swamp rock example outside of the United States to that point.

'Come Down in Time' (Elton John, Bernie Taupin)

Released as a single A-side, 1971 (Philippines), b/w 'Love Song'.
A totally different colour palette is employed here. Appearing out-of-step with the American west concept as a whole, but passed over for the *Elton*

John album, this mellow jazz-inflected piece was now enlivened by Paul Buckmaster's shimmering orchestral arrangement, cementing its worthiness for inclusion here.

Underpinning the glassy atmosphere was Blue Mink drummer Barry Morgan, effectively providing modernity through a syncopated feel, accompanied by the swoops of double-bassist, Chris Laurence. Also noteworthy was an early appearance on oboe by Welsh composer, Karl Jenkins.

But artists covering the song failed to let it breathe, over-complicating their arrangements by varying tempos, rhythmic patterns and chords, not to mention annihilating Elton's original and poignant ending chord which was a high-point in the first place. Such was the case with the overcooked version by Eugene Pitt and the Jyve Fyve. A version by American keyboardist Al Kooper was better but ravaged by a marginally flat-pitched Mellotron, though the second-verse percussion groove was tastefully executed.

Mention must be made of Sting's 1991 version from the *Two Rooms: Celebrating the Songs of Elton John & Bernie Taupin* tribute album, which remained faithful to the original in spite of the fact Sting appended the line 'Come down in time was the message she gave' with the words 'to me'. The ending, happily intact, nevertheless included the major third in the final chord, where the original had followed Buckmaster's habit of leaving the third out of a closing orchestral chord, as evidenced in both 'I Need You to Turn To' and 'The King Must Die'.

'Country Comfort' (Elton John, Bernie Taupin)

Released as a single A-side, 1971 (AUS and NZ), b/w 'Love Song'.

An obvious choice for a single, maybe this lyric's praise of an idyllic rural existence interrupted by inevitable industrialisation was considered a bit cumbersome for the charts and only relevant to some.

The recording marked the debut on an Elton record, of future live band mainstay, bassist Dee Murray, albeit on backing vocals only here along with Nigel Olsson. Issued as a single in Australasia, both sides received airplay but failed to chart.

Silver Metre included the carelessly re-titled 'Country Comforts' on their 1969 self-titled album, replete with many a lyrical faux-pas. Three months prior to the UK release of *Tumbleweed*, Rod Stewart recorded 'Country Comfort' for his *Gasoline Alley* album in a rhythmically plodding performance where he appeared to be recalling the lyrics from memory (a recurring theme). But British psychedelic pop band Orange Bicycle offered up a far superior and positive-sounding take on this hit-that-should-have-been.

The basic track for Elton's version was recorded when he was away in Holland. Pianist Peter Robinson filled in for Elton who overdubbed his playing on the track when he got back. The song was a respectable stab at the country genre if a tad clumsy in lyrical detail if we consider that the hedgehog is not native to the USA. The word 'porcupine' may not have scanned the same, but the idea had to get through. After all, Bernie has stated that it was Marty Robbins' 1959 hit 'El Paso' that made him want to write songs, so the country influence was bound to find its way to the surface of Elton's material in one way or another before the pair had set foot in America.

'Son of Your Father' (Elton John, Bernie Taupin)

This tale of two friends who kill each other in a fight is given energy by the funky precision of the rhythm section; drummer Roger Pope, bassist Dave Glover and ever-present guitarist Caleb Quaye. The song also cemented through repetition what would become the 'Goodbye Yellow Brick Road' intro descending chord pattern, which makes itself known at 0m:48s. Originally stated just once in 'The Greatest Discovery' on the *Elton John* album, this chord motif was to reappear sporadically throughout Elton's repertoire.

Three months before the release of *Tumbleweed*, UK rock band Spooky Tooth recorded a slower but more rock-edged version for their album, The Last Puff, but failing to attract as many cover versions as some of its album-mates, 'Son of Your Father' probably suffered by default from being a good song surrounded by superior material.

'My Father's Gun' (Elton John, Bernie Taupin)

In this poignant ballad, Bernie gave us a Confederate soldier in an American Civil War battle. He buries his father in the south, takes his gun and returns to the fight, dreaming of a time when the battle is over, and he can go home.

The repeating chorus play-out section is mesmerising. The backing vocals cry out and Buckmaster's tastefully understated arrangement sets the scene with horns and low strings eventually creeping in to unsettle the situation further. Caleb Quaye adds to the intensity with chaotic jazz guitar licks galloping through the scene.

The musical simplicity and lyrical clarity of this piece communicates a feeling of frustration with the senselessness of war, in a fashion more instantly accessible to the listener than almost anything on the *Elton John* album – simplicity and clarity being characteristics that would distinguish many future Elton ballads.

'Where To Now St Peter' (Elton John, Bernie Taupin)

It's easy to imagine this being the same character from 'My Father's Gun', taking an opportunity for some kind of reprieve from the insanity, but resorting to beseech St Peter, despite a lack of religious faith. Another interpretation and probably closer to the truth is that the faithless character has died and is asking for direction at the pearly gates. Or you could simply consider the lyric as more Bernie psychedelia with religious overtones fitting alongside 'Hymn 2000', or more 'Empty Sky' incarceration, except this time of a psychological nature.

However, you view it, this upbeat recording harks back to the simplicity of *Empty Sky* songs like 'Lady, What's Tomorrow' and 'Sails', but like the rest of

Tumbleweed, benefits from the newly improved production and arrangement. This comparison is understandable in light of the fact that the *Elton John* and *Tumbleweed* songs were written contemporary to each other, some coming from earlier. There was so much material around at this point that the album was even slated to be a double at one stage.

'Where To Now St Peter' provided another potential single for the virtually single-less *Tumbleweed Connection* and, with the help of several other tracks, gave the album a welcome contrast against the darker but well-meaning ballads.

'Love Song' (Lesley Duncan)
Released as a single A-side, 1971 (France), b/w 'Empty Sky (Edit)'.
Released as a single B-side, 1971 (AUS and NZ), b/w 'Country Comfort'.
Released as a single B-side, 1971 (Philippines), b/w 'Come Down in Time'.
Elton was a fan of pop singer Lesley Duncan in the '60s, from her own records and those of Dusty Springfield with Lesley as backing vocalist. Elton knew her from backing vocal sessions they had both worked on.

After Lesley sang in the vocal group on *Elton John*, Elton asked to record a song of hers, and they settled on 'Love Song'. Two acoustic guitars played by Lesley, followed by multiple vocal overdubs from her and Elton and it was done. A final touch was the beachside sound effects thrown in the middle, giving the lyric a broader conceptual arc suggesting the idea of love as being more than confined to a romantic relationship. A simple and effective, if lightweight pop song, 'Love Song' sits perhaps slightly out-of-place on *Tumbleweed Connection* but brings welcome relief amongst the comparatively heavier material. Its inclusion also speaks volumes for Elton as a fan of, and mentor for, other artists.

DJM issued 'Love Song' as a single in France with an edited version of 'Empty Sky' on the B-side. This would quite possibly be one of the more collectable Elton singles in existence.

'Amoreena' (Elton John, Bernie Taupin)
The delicious love song 'Amoreena' is widely regarded as quintessential Elton of the time.His recording was a landmark, being the debut of drummer Nigel Olsson and bassist Dee Murray together instrumentally on an Elton track. The solid and singular interplay of the three here, especially in the closing verse, is a clear forerunner of the dynamic live powerhouse the trio would become playing England, parts of the continent, and North America later in 1970.

A fascinating cover of the song was released by British group Panhandle on their one-off self-titled album in 1972. It featured *Tumbleweed* session players Barry Morgan and Herbie Flowers, and percussionist Dennis Lopez who had appeared on *Elton John*. But most surprising was the addition of comedian and jazz pianist Dudley Moore, who gave an oddly unsure rendition of the part. Panhandle's performance is lifted almost note for note (but not word for word, again!) from Elton's, but is less impactful – his version being a hard act to follow.

The strength of 'Amoreena' was recognised when used for the opening of the 1975 Al Pacino movie, *Dog Day Afternoon*. But it was not the first Elton track to be used in a movie it wasn't written for. That honour went to 'Daniel' in the 1974 movie, *Alice Doesn't Live Here Anymore*.

'Talking Old Soldiers' (Elton John, Bernie Taupin)

This dynamic and dramatic solo piano and voice ballad is the most lucid track on *Tumbleweed Connection*. Inspired by American singer/songwriter David Ackles, the emotive conversation between what could be either two Civil War soldiers or World War veterans makes its point and is gone, like the friends the narrator mourns. For pure composition-meets-performance, this neglected gem likely trumps everything else on the album.

'Burn Down the Mission' (Elton John, Bernie Taupin)

Never ones to pass up an opportunity for musical tension or drama, Elton and co took full advantage of the final six minutes and twenty seconds of the album with this dynamic tour-de-force, not only in general musically, but as a formal path-forger for future material.

The work of New York singer/songwriter Laura Nyro was a formal influence on the song. Her unconventional approach to standard pop song forms by having a more open, flowing, changeable and unpredictable movement through a song, had an influence on many songwriters of the time. Elton demonstrated this here with the middle section tempo increase, key changes and a dynamic back-and-forth trajectory. This technique would be repeated on future Elton tracks such as 'Madman Across the Water', 'Love Lies Bleeding' and the 1973 re-recording of 'Grey Seal'.

Some have described this lyric as being enigmatic, resurrecting as it does an idea from their 1968 song 'The Angel Tree'. The narrator appears to be disillusioned, seeing no recourse but to destroy his community's symbol of faith, after which he is simply taken away. To me, the message is clear enough to balance evenly with the changeable top surface.

Tumbleweed Connection was Bernie and Elton at their most conceptually cinematic to this point – a multi-layered wide-shot conceptual collage of New World political and religious concerns.

Friends (Soundtrack) (1971)

Personnel:
Elton John: vocals, piano
Leslie Duncan, Mike Egan, Caleb Quaye, Les Thatcher: acoustic guitar
Madeline Bell, Lesley Duncan, Liza Strike: backing vocals
Dee Murray, Alan Weighill: bass
Barry Morgan, Nigel Olsson: drums
Caleb Quaye: guitar
Rex Morris: tenor sax
Recorded: Sept./Oct. 1970 at Trident Studios, London
Producer: Gus Dudgeon
Engineer: Robin Geoffrey Cable
Arranger: Paul Buckmaster
Release date: April 1971 (UK), 5 March 1971 (US)
Chart placings: UK: did not chart, US: 36

Elton made his triumphant first trip to America in August 1970 before
recording for *Friends* commenced back in London at Trident in late September.
The movie soundtrack had to be completed before Elton returned to America
for three Boston Tea Party concerts scheduled from 29 October.

His stateside hit with 'Your Song' probably aided the *Friends* soundtrack in
the level of success it achieved, being certified gold on the first day of shipping,
despite the fact the 500,000 discs were all sent back. But the soundtrack was
eventually nominated for Best Original Score at the 1972 Grammy Awards and
the film itself for Best English Language Foreign Film at the Golden Globes.

Elton and Bernie originally signed an agreement to write just three
songs for the movie. Two extra songs, 'Honey Roll' and 'Can I Put You On',
shared the 'Amoreena' line-up of Quaye, Murray and Olsson, and similarly
demonstrated the quartet's deftness with a funky groove. These were not
written or recorded specifically for the movie, and Elton later regretted not
saving them for his own albums.

Add to the recipe the poignant ballad 'Seasons' and the album must be
considered essential listening for the hardcore fan. It's fair to say that the high
point of the soundtrack was arranger Paul Buckmaster's sumptuously cello-laden
eleven-minute incidental epic, 'Four Moods', which alone was worth the price of
admission. The title track was a Top 40 hit single in the USA in April 1971.

'Friends' (Elton John, Bernie Taupin)

Released as a single A-side, 23 April 1971 (UK), 5 March 1971 (US), b/w 'Honey
Roll'. US: 34. CAN: 13. AUS: 96. NZ: 19.
A smaller production than 'Your Song', but with a more emotive chord
progression, Elton's second US hit single was superior in its pure pop melody
but lacked the bigger hit's lyrical innovation and clearly also its ability to grab
the public by the jugular. A non-starter on the UK singles chart, it reached

34 in *Billboard* but got as high 17 in *Cashbox*, its stateside success therefore measured by where the chart-stat gatherers' loyalties lay.

'Honey Roll' (Elton John, Bernie Taupin)

Released as a single B-side, 23 April 1971 (UK), 5 March 1971 (US), b/w 'Friends'. An encore of sorts to 'Amoreena' due to the reappearance of the Quaye/Murray/ Olsson band line-up, 'Honey Roll' shines thanks to tasteful musical interplay from a tight drums/bass/piano unit who were now a well-oiled machine fresh from the road. Elton's playing was metronomic, minus drums for the first 30 seconds, teasing us with the funky gospel of those left-hand octaves.

The central sax solo was an interesting addition, certainly, in its second half where two takes were simultaneously audible, neither of them satisfactory, suggesting time was of the essence. The lyric too was light, and along with the sax solo likely scuppered the song's consideration for an official Elton album, but not for the B-side of the 'Friends' single.

'Seasons' (Elton John, Bernie Taupin)

With the whiff of a potential classic about it, this brief piano and orchestra ballad bore a melodic similarity to 'Country Comfort' and pre-empted the melancholy mood of the coming *Madman Across the Water*. With side projects being a good opportunity to experiment and/or solve problems to some extent, perhaps this neglected child was the best reminder to iron out the habit of repetitive vocal trills that Elton fell into for a couple of years there.

'Can I Put You On' (Elton John, Bernie Taupin)

The initial striking tremolo guitar here sounds like it was cleverly added after the fact to spice up the introduction. It has such personality that it could have quite conceivably spawned an entire genre. It's a shame the flavour was not integrated into the track more.

With the same band line-up as 'Honey Roll', this more rock-edged funk outing shone thanks to guitarist Caleb Quaye's subtle Hendrix-isms, but sadly came off a tad unbalanced with a 2m:45s semi-sing-along coda that was an opportunity for some blistering soloing that failed to appear.

The lyric's story of northern workers conveniently fit the film but wasn't written for it, unless Bernie changed a word or two after the fact. Either way, the lyric seemed rushed and in need of more work, but I'd guess that Elton and Bernie were hardly going to loan their best material to a side project.

Ultimately, 'Can I Put You On' was more befitting the live situation, as would soon be heard on the *17-11-70* live album.

'Michelle's Song' (Elton John, Bernie Taupin)

Functional but sounding like a backward step, 'Michelle's Song', specially written for the film, occupied an oboe-laden soft rock zone. In 1971 this could have qualified it as a second single. But the harmonic promise of the verse failed to blossom into a chorus with a hook strong enough to hang your hat on.

17-11-70 (Live) (UK)/11-17-70 (Live) (USA) (1971)

Personnel:
Elton John: vocals, piano
Dee Murray: fretless bass, vocals
Nigel Olsson: drums, vocals
Recorded: 17 November 1970 at A & R Recording Studios, New York
Producer: Gus Dudgeon
Engineer: Phil Ramone
Release date: April 1971 (UK), 10 May 1971 (US)
Chart placings: UK: 20, US: 11, CAN: 10

Track choice for the original live *17-11-70* vinyl album seems to have been based purely on vocal performance, which of course made perfect sense. In such a situation, any instrumental flubs can be passed off as intentional, if discernible at all, but the human voice by its very nature is not always reliable. Therefore, track selection for a live album was at the mercy of nature to an extent, at least in 1971 with the technology then available.

The performance was recorded in front of an audience of 100 that crammed into Phil Ramone's A & R Studios (formerly Columbia) in Manhattan. Being simultaneously broadcast live on WABC FM, the band wore headphones. But Elton didn't realise it was being recorded, thinking it was only to be broadcast. Not originally intended for a live album, DJM released *17-11-70* due to bootlegs of the FM radio broadcast hitting the streets.

The 1995 Mercury reissue remixed by Gus Dudgeon, improved the sound enormously. Ambient delay was added to piano and vocal in spots, and a warm flanging effect added to some bass parts. 'Amoreena' was an additional bonus track.

In hindsight, the unsung star of the show has to be Dee Murray's bass performance which shone with a clearly unbridled love of rhythm and blues, which wasn't always evident from his recorded Elton output. Murray was virtually matchless when he let fly in that mode, which he clearly committed to later on parts of Elton's '80s albums like *Jump Up* and *Too Low for Zero*.

The 2017 double vinyl reissue titled *17-11-70+* added a second disc featuring the remaining unreleased tracks from the concert, so we'll examine the entire set-list here, but in its originally performed sequence.

It's interesting to note that back in this time period, any piano Elton touched magically assumed his unique tone and character. Even the Steinway recorded here, previously heard on Dionne Warwick's Burt Bacharach-produced hits, and suffering from a low-register tuning issue at the recording of *17-11-70*, succumbed to Elton's touch. It's something to do with his signature chord formation technique which often spanned a complete octave.

17-11-70 is a historic artefact that shed light on the sheer abilities of all the musicians involved, who were on the cusp of an intense touring and recording schedule that would span the next four years.

'I Need You to Turn To' (Elton John, Bernie Taupin)

It took a couple of songs for Elton to warm up, with no help from the fact he couldn't hear his voice in the headphones, going by the comment he made after the song. Nevertheless, this was a fair voice and piano rendition of the moody *Elton John* ballad.

'Your Song' (Elton John, Bernie Taupin)

This was better - piano and voice only, with the added touch of bassist Dee Murray joining in on the outro. Elton was still having monitoring problems, with the piano now being too loud in the headphones, but at the end, after he gave a short band introduction, the show began for real.

'Country Comfort' (Elton John, Bernie Taupin)

After the minor sound problems, the full band now kicked in with a bang. Elton's voice was instantly in fine form, proving the function of the first two songs as Elton's soundcheck. The song came to life with a vigour it lacked in its *Tumbleweed Connection* recording. This was a funk exercise from the one-minute-mark entry of Nigel and Dee, and a quality workout it was. The *Tumbleweed* recording of 'Country Comfort' would have been vastly improved by the use of this powerhouse rhythm section.

'Border Song' (Elton John, Bernie Taupin)

The second verse of 'Border Song' was beautifully enhanced by the eerie quality of Dee Murray's weeping bass volume work. When the full band broke out over the bridge and last verse, their natural funk leanings complimented this gospel outing perfectly. On finishing, Elton quipped that they'd played the song so often that they now called it the 'Boredom Song'.

'Indian Sunset' (Elton John, Bernie Taupin)

It was still nine months before 'Indian Sunset' was to be recorded for the *Madman Across the Water* album, so I'll save any compositional description for when we get there. Suffice to say, the song section format here is virtually intact, but minus the band cues that may have come about as a consequence of Paul Buckmaster's eventual arrangement. The instrumental link from the first verse to the middle section was certainly lengthened on *Madman* from how it is played here.

This is a fine and historically interesting solo piano and voice performance of a landmark song from Elton's early repertoire. Surely only its length prevented its inclusion on the original vinyl edition of *17-11-70*.

'Amoreena' (Elton John, Bernie Taupin)

Similarity and slight inferiority to the *Tumbleweed Connection* version of 'Amoreena' possibly determined this live recording's fateful omission from the original *17-11-70* album. It was first Released as a bonus track added to the 1996 Rocket Records reissue.

'Bad Side of the Moon' (Elton John, Bernie Taupin)

Perfectly suited to live performance, this 'Border Song' B-side had now found another home, morphing from psychedelic orchestra liquid to tight, punchy, crowd-pleasing concert staple. Not bad going for a rarity, proving there was more to Elton than mere hit singles and strings of delectable deep-cuts.

'Take Me to the Pilot' (Elton John, Bernie Taupin)

Elton's piano part here had developed considerably from the comparative simplicity of the *Elton John* recording, through a string of concert dates in Europe and the USA, arriving at a rock piano solo taking up the entire second half of this performance. Just when you think the band are steaming towards the end, they pull back for a subtle but dynamic joint improvisation before ploughing through a final play-out section to finish. *This* was live music in 1970. No tricks, no machines, no net. Just a three-piece band live on a highwire.

'Sixty Years On' (Elton John, Bernie Taupin)

The transformation here from intense orchestral statement to three-piece rock band performance seemed remarkably effortless, like one of those situations where you don't know it can't be done. The song retained all the intensity and drive diverted through the prism.

Gus Dudgeon's 1995 remix blurs the piano intro with echo delay, although it does sound good when applied to the vocal in selected spots.

'Honky Tonk Women' (Mick Jagger, Keith Richards)

A seemingly unnecessary addition to the band's repertoire, the a-cappella vocal harmony introduction to this Rolling Stones cover alone demonstrates the musical skill these three musicians possessed. All are perfectly in tune, and Dee Murray's vocal part especially has a large mid-line upward jump that would challenge the most seasoned of singers. Where many backing vocalists might take the easy way by moving through a momentarily shared unison note to make life easier, these guys did things right. Again, it was a mark of the times.

'Can I Put You On' (Elton John, Bernie Taupin)

As with much of *17-11-70*, the star here is Dee Murray's bass-playing. Gus Dudgeon's remix adds a bonus silvery sheen of flanger which beautifies the bass tone immensely. Elsewhere, Murray anticipates by a few years, the bubbling lines of future fretless bass luminary Jaco Pastorius.

'Burn Down the Mission' (Elton John, Bernie Taupin)
Including: 'My Baby Left Me' (Arthur Crudup) and 'Get Back'
(Paul McCartney)

In many ways, the concert finale is also the cornerstone of the show. It covers all the bases, first with the grand statement that is 'Burn Down the Mission', followed by a dynamic eleven-minute jam that illuminates the talents of all onstage. In the remix, Gus Dudgeon added a subtle lower octave to beef up the bass solo, to tremendous effect.

Incorporating the rockabilly standard, 'My Baby Left Me', and The Beatles' 'Get Back', the eighteen-minute outpouring then winds down to a spoken thank you over the band, then back up to a rousing finish.

'My Father's Gun' (Elton John, Bernie Taupin)

The encore of 'My Father's Gun' wended its way uneventfully but perfectly adequately to its end. The high points of the show had passed. The show's performances of 'Indian Sunset' and 'Burn Down the Mission' were hard acts to follow for any other piece.

Madman Across the Water (1971)

Personnel:
Elton John: vocals, piano
Jack Emblow: accordion
Tony Burrows, Roger Cook, Lesley Duncan, Dee Murray, Nigel Olsson, Terry Steele,
Barry St. John, Liza Strike, Sue & Sunny: backing vocals
Chris Laurence: acoustic bass
Herbie Flowers, David Glover, Dee Murray, Brian Odgers: bass
Cantores in Ecclesia directed by Robert Kirby: choir
Terry Cox, Barry Morgan, Nigel Olsson, Roger Pope: drums
Davey Johnstone, Les Thatcher: acoustic guitar
Caleb Quaye, Chris Spedding: electric guitar
Brian Dee: harmonium
Davey Johnstone: mandolin
Rick Wakeman: organ
Ray Cooper: percussion
Davey Johnstone: sitar
B.J. Cole: steel guitar
Diana Lewis: synthesizer
Recorded: 27 Feb. & 9, 11 and 14 Aug. 1971 at Trident Studios, London
Producer: Gus Dudgeon
Engineer: Robin Geoffrey Cable
Arranger: Paul Buckmaster
Release date: 5 Nov. 1971 (UK), 15 Nov. 1971 (US)
Chart placings: UK: 41, US: 8, CAN: 9, AUS: 8

Elton's fourth official studio album was recorded under pressure, and incredibly, within only four days in February and August 1971. The following gives an idea of Elton's tight schedule at the time. He and the band performed a concert at Brunel University in Uxbridge on the night of Friday 26 February. The following day he recorded 'Levon' and 'Goodbye' at Trident Studios in London, before hightailing it up to Yorkshire for a concert that night at Bradford University.

More UK dates and a full American tour ensued across the summer, before a couple of European dates including Vilar Dos Mouros, Portugal, on the night of Sunday 8 August. The following day, Elton reconvened at Trident with Pope, Glover and Quaye to record 'Tiny Dancer', 'Razor Face' and 'Holiday Inn'. Added to the line-up that day was Magna Carta guitarist Davey Johnstone, who would soon join Elton's live band and go on to contribute to every Elton album until 1978, thereafter re-establishing his presence on 1983's *Too Low for Zero*.

On Wednesday 11 August came the recording of 'All the Nasties', historic for the coming together of Olsson, Murray, and newcomer, percussionist Ray Cooper. This was the closest incarnation yet to what would become Elton's more fleshed-out live band, albeit minus Davey Johnstone for this session.

Add to this the presence of the Cantores in Ecclesia choir for the gospel vocal touches, and you have a pretty good practice run for the extreme single day of Saturday 14 August which would witness the recording of 'Rotten Peaches', 'Madman Across the Water' and 'Indian Sunset', replete with orchestra.

With 'Tiny Dancer' and 'Holiday Inn' we had an additional partial future band sneak preview, as those recordings featured Roger Pope, Caleb Quaye and Davey Johnstone together, who would reconvene in 1975 for *Rock of the Westies*. Also, take into account the minefield of other session players on this album, and you have a pretty broad selection of not only Elton '70s alumni, but that of the current 1971 London recording scene in general. There may have been a feeling that the sessions, with their sheer number of personnel, were getting out of control. 1972's *Honky Chateau* would certainly be a streamlining, but first, we have the *Madman* monster with which to contend.

'Tiny Dancer' (Elton John, Bernie Taupin)
Released as a single A-side, 7 February 1972 (US and CAN), b/w 'Razor Face'. US: 41. CAN: 19.
Released as a double A-side single, May 1972 (AUS), b/w 'Rocket Man'. AUS: 13.
The opening piano chords of 'Tiny Dancer' are harmonically similar to those of 'Country Comfort' but sound more expansive. Where *Tumbleweed Connection* was sonically intimate and in your face, *Madman Across the Water* is sweeping and widespread, featuring a large cast of session players similar to the *Elton John* album. 'Tiny Dancer' has the honour of being the first Elton record to feature guitarist Davey Johnstone, who would subsequently leave his group Magna Carta to augment Elton's live band.

In the USA, the single, the second from *Madman*, peaked at 41 on the chart despite airplay of a radio-friendly 3m:45s edit ending after the first double chorus, which virtually halved the track's length. This short version was released that year as a double A-side with 'Rocket Man' in parts of Europe and in Australia where it had more success, reaching number 13. There was no UK single issue.

Dedicated to Bernie Taupin's girlfriend Maxine Feibelman, the lyric is often misconstrued as being completely about her. It was, in addition, a more general observation of the open cultural spirit of California that awaited any visitor, not least of all a rock entourage. The Jesus freaks handing tickets out in the street were a striking L.A. image against the ballerina dancing in the sand, not to mention the subtle innuendo of the individuals waiting on rock royalty. It was all there, and it was all in the lyric, if softened by a bed of pedal steel guitar, courtesy of British session player B.J. Cole.

Ex Brasil '66 vocalist Lani Hall covered the song on her 1972 album *Sun Down Lady* in a tame rendering that unnecessarily skewed the lyrics to an outsider's perspective, observing the man observing the woman. Along the way a lyric rearrangement from 'The words she knows, The tune she hums', to the absurd 'The tune she knows, The words she hums', continued the apparent growing tradition of cover singers failing to correctly research Bernie's lyrics – a discovery which this book sheds light upon by default.

'Levon' (Elton John, Bernie Taupin)

Released as a single A-side, 29 November 1971 (US), b/w 'Goodbye'. US: 24. CAN: 6.
Released as a single A-side, March 1972 (AUS and NZ), b/w 'Sails'. AUS: 94.

More lyrically abstract and instrumentally impactful than the former song, the first-released *Madman* single kicks the album on its way in a cacophony of cinematic imagery, whining harmonium and forthright cello statements. Subtle in the first song, Paul Buckmaster's signature string moves make themselves unapologetically known here starting from the dramatic build-up to the first chorus.

At this stage, I was almost afraid to research contemporary cover versions. I decided against holding my breath in hopes of finding a cover with lyrics intact. It was the right decision. American gospel singer Mary McCreary recorded a respectable version of 'Levon' for her 1974 album *Jezebel*. But as if by magic, we arrive at the line 'Sits on the porch swing watching them fly', only to be greeted with 'sits on the porch swing watching balloons go by' – a clumsy substitute by anyone's standard. And instead of 'Take a balloon and go sailing', we get 'Takes up a ship and goes sailing'. It's a perplexing but perhaps telling phenomenon that exposes an aspect of the commercial record business often prevalent even then; Do it fast, get it done, get it out.

According to Bernie, the lyric is the simple tale of a guy who wants to escape from the hold his father has over him. But there is much more to be gleaned as the ample detail allows you to climb right inside the story and walk around. The guy who wants to escape is actually Levon's son Jesus who appears to be trapped in the thriving family business. Jesus' grandfather Alvin was apparently newsworthy enough for Levon's Christmas birth to have been mentioned in the New York Times, thereby establishing the presence of some kind of historic family success and therefore an eventual level of expectation on poor old Jesus.

It's quite a concoction, with enough detail to make a good movie, enough surely to take care in a cover recording, and more than enough to set up quite an expectation for whatever the rest of the album had to offer.

'Razor Face' (Elton John, Bernie Taupin)

After being seduced by funky introductory piano anticipations similar to 'Honey Roll', what you get here is a folk-rock outing a la The Band, that wouldn't be out of place on *Tumbleweed Connection*. The virtuosic accordion soloing of Jack Emblow over the play-out section certainly lends itself to that feeling, as do the lines simultaneously chiselled from Caleb Quaye's fretboard. The SACD version of the album extends the song with two extra minutes of carefree play-out solo providing, along with 'Holiday Inn', some radiance to an album with an otherwise widely overcast setting.

Unfortunately, the strong melody and memorable hooks failed to attract cover versions, possibly due to the abstract nature of the lyrics which masked the meaning to an extent. But considering how fast and loose cover singers were with Bernie's lyrics anyway, would it have really mattered? But that's the beauty of a song like this - we don't necessarily need the story to be tied up in a bow with a payoff line. The popular theory of 'Razor Face' being about a Vietnam veteran is one possibility, though World War I is probably more like it if you go by the line, 'Must be getting on, Needs a man who's young to walk him 'round'.

Further lyrical nuances such as unexpected perspective changes, confounded the clarity. Bernie often displayed similar techniques, as if playing devil's advocate with the guidelines laid down by a prior generation of pop lyricists who'd set the bar extremely high. After all, without traffic lights, the road would be mere chaos. But by 1971, all lyricists had the spectre of Bob Dylan's exact, though often obtuse, lyrical practices leering over their shoulder, as if daring them to take risks – risks you'd need a stuntman for, Dylan being, according to many, the single individual capable of pulling off such stunts.

But I doubt Bernie gave this kind of competition or definition of technique too much thought. The lyric is still fresh and alive regardless - unencumbered by the pedantic, and largely open to interpretation.

'Madman Across the Water' (Elton John, Bernie Taupin)

Speaking of overcast, the manic title song gave the most glorious promise of perpetual rainfall on an Elton track yet. The clouds gather from the outset with meandering piano clusters hemmed in by backward reverberated acoustic guitar accents as a harbinger of the storm to come.

The lyric was mysterious, but the claim that it referred to Richard Nixon was untrue, Bernie later saying it was about an asylum. But the sheer musicality here, in the orchestral arrangement alone, must surely trump the lyric in the attention-getting stakes.

The pressure to complete the album was certainly recognized in the recording of this song. On one scheduled day, presumably either Thursday 12 August or Friday 13 August, a 60-piece orchestra sat waiting to record, Paul Buckmaster then arriving with no score. The track was ultimately cut on the final recording day of Saturday 14 August 1971. The result carried a tense and dramatic string arrangement with many impressive moments, such as the aggressive angular section that enters at 2m:21s, and the motivating but unsettling polyrhythmic triplet five-note statement that closes the final chorus at 4m:29s. Not to forget the Ligeti-esque string liquid that creates 20 seconds of tension from 4m:40s, using a similar technique to the buzzing introduction of 'Sixty Years On'. And all this is just the orchestra.

Elsewhere, Elton's angry biting vocal and Davey Johnstone's high cutting guitar harmonics provide a startling contrast to Diana Lewis' sinewy low synthesizer lines and the primal poundings of new addition, percussionist

Ray Cooper, who'd entered the fold on the 'All the Nasties' session three days before.

As a whole it's a huge development forward from the original timid version of the song recorded for *Tumbleweed Connection*, featuring David Bowie guitarist Mick Ronson. That version did, however, make interesting use of atmospheric guitar effects that could have made further momentary enhancements to this new recording. But the producer knew when to stop. 'Madman Across the Water' is a landmark in Elton's repertoire - a six-minute act that could only be successfully followed by the even longer, more expansively cinematic and story-driven masterstroke, 'Indian Sunset'.

'Indian Sunset' (Elton John, Bernie Taupin)

For anyone familiar with 'Indian Sunset' from having been present at the 17-11-70 concert or having had possession of a contemporary bootleg of the performance, the initial release of the song, which was a cover version by former Peter, Paul and Mary member Mary Travers, would have been a definite item of interest. Thanks to a flute-laden middle-of-the-road atmosphere and some lyric perspective-fiddling, the song was presented from more of a lightweight story-telling angle, Luckily, this adventurous undertaking on Travers' part was immune from comparison, Elton's live performance being unreleased, and coming a full six months before he even recorded the studio version, which hypothetically saved Travers some considerable face. That way the criticism would have been slanted more towards the appearance of a substantial new John/Taupin composition on the market, as opposed to an inferior cover, which would have been in real danger of being perceived as a B-grade TV western next to Elton's widescreen cinematography.

In some ways, Elton's live solo version was pure and unaffected enough as to render an orchestral arrangement superfluous, so it is to arranger Paul Buckmaster's credit that he served only to enhance the inherently cinematic piece. In the hands of a lesser arranger, this lengthy multi-section opus could have been seen as an opportunity to jettison all limitation and lapse into excess, but 'Sixty Years On' had already given a taste of Buckmaster with the brakes off, him later tellingly referring to it as his '30s horror movie'. The recording of 'Indian Sunset' may have been too soon in the timeline for him to yet reach that conclusion about 'Sixty Years On', but in contrast to it, 'Indian Sunset' had a lucid lyric carrying the entire thing, which made staying out of the way a no-brainer.

Easing the listener into side two, the moves were subtle indeed. A soft sustained chord of orchestral strings with a slight phasing effect set the scene to introduce the first verse solo vocal – horns then creeping in followed by a repetitive warlike drum pattern. Later, melodic string lines highlighted the instrumental sections, but with nothing as dissonant or disturbing as those in the title track. Throw in some rhythmic accents to close the two band sections, and that was pretty much it. No grand statements.

It was all about the lyric, which was the tale of an American Indian warrior who takes his family and follows the yellow moon in search of vengeance. Along the way, he learns of Geronimo's death, fictionalised here as a murder, which only heightens the overall dramatic effect. Lyrical liberties like this caused some critics to sneer, but this was merely art – Bernie wasn't writing a history book. The climax arrived with the ambiguous death of the warrior himself. Whether it was murder or suicide was left to the listener's imagination.

Adventurous yes, but probably not the most progressive Elton track - that honour would most likely be reserved for the 1973 instrumental 'Funeral for a Friend' - but 'Indian Sunset' was perhaps his most artistically ambitious, at least for its period. Combine that with a characteristic simplicity that some of its companion songs lacked, and with 'Indian Sunset' you have an early-period pinnacle.

'Holiday Inn' (Elton John, Bernie Taupin)

Released as a single B-side, April 1972 (UK), b/w 'Rocket Man'.
In this lyric, Elton and Bernie's recent personal discovery of the USA was close to the surface. Like 'Tiny Dancer', it shared observations of being on the road – general mostly, but specific to the hotel chain in question in the below third verse removed from the recording.

> *Don't even know if it's Cleveland or Maine*
> *Well the building's as big*
> *And the room's just the same*
> *Oh the TV don't work, and the French fries are cold*
> *And room service closed 'bout an hour ago*

The instrumentation had the mandolin-led feel of a folk-rock track, again suggesting The Band as a reference. The instrumental mid-section was augmented by a psychedelic combination of Indian-sounding violin swoops and sitar – Davey Johnstone playing the latter instrument, here making its debut on an Elton recording, not to be resurrected until 1972's *Don't Shoot Me I'm Only the Piano Player* track, 'Blues For Baby and Me'.

Listening today, 'Holiday Inn' fulfils the function of clearing the air after the preceding dramas. More dramatic attempts follow, but side two never really regains momentum after its opening showstopper.

'Rotten Peaches' (Elton John, Bernie Taupin)

Straddling country and blues in that stylistic soup that Elton was now so adept at cooking up, the focus here was on the lyric. The narrator, a prisoner of the US state system, laments his days on the chain gang and on the sea, along with his perpetual exposure to dead fruit, both literal and metaphorical.

Instrumental details sweetened proceedings with tasteful synthesizer lines from Diana Lewis and slide guitar from Chris Spedding. An interesting aspect after the fact is how the chorus thematically anticipates 1973's 'Have Mercy on the Criminal'. So fitting the album perfectly, 'Rotten Peaches' was steeped in dark subject matter, and oddly, dark matter somehow deemed fit for a full minute of repetitive sing-along refrain a la The Beatles' 'Hey Jude', to take the song out.

'All the Nasties' (Elton John, Bernie Taupin)

This lyric took an unexpected turn towards the confessional. In an abstract way, it expressed Bernie's attitude towards early-career criticism, journalistic or otherwise. The line, 'If they could turn their focus off to the image in their eyes', basically said it all, and fitting the predictable unpredictability of public and professional opinion, the verse chords travelled in a non-linear fashion, never quite landing where you might expect.

The chords accompanying the line, 'Turn a full-blooded city boy into a full-blooded city man', repeated in several places minus the vocals, to reveal a striking similarity to the 'Take Me to the Pilot' introduction - even in the same key. I'd guess this move was subconscious, but either way, it was irrelevant. Many composers have spread motifs amongst their compositions, whether by design or not – a practice that upon discovery only enriches the listening process.

To the casual observer, the inscrutable 'All the Nasties' was in danger of coming off as self-indulgent. It was so difficult to get to the bottom of and was compounded by no mention of the title in the lyric, nor any defined hook to orientate the listener. These are, of course, valid compositional choices, but ones that can leave a listener perplexed.

The ending though appeared to be an attempt to correct the above problem. The repetitive sing-along technique used in the prior song was hauled out again, but the entire gospel choir aspect seemed anchorless and minus a reason to be present. The interminable sing-along refrain with its aimless exclamation of 'Oh my soul' inhabited the song's entire second half, paradoxically weighing it down, like the ending of 'Rotten Peaches' but on steroids.

An oddity in the Elton repertoire, 'All the Nasties' redeems itself through historical interest, being the closest incarnation yet of Elton's coming touring band of Nigel Olsson, Dee Murray and percussionist Ray Cooper together, albeit minus Davey Johnstone.

'Goodbye' (Elton John, Bernie Taupin)

Released as a single B-side, April 1972 (UK), b/w 'Rocket Man'.
Released as a single B-side, 29 November 1971 (US), b/w 'Levon'.
Hovering on the edge of sentimentality but failing to tumble right in, this finely cut solo voice and piano miniature is sublime in its combination of explanation and mystery.

Honky Chateau (1972)

Personnel:
Elton John: vocals, pianos, organ
Madeleine Bell, Gus Dudgeon, Tony Hazzard, Davey Johnstone, Dee Murray, Nigel Olsson, Larry Steel, Liza Strike: backing vocals
Dee Murray: bass
Nigel Olsson: drums
Jean-Luc Ponty: electric violin
Davey Johnstone: guitar, banjo, mandolin
Ray Cooper, Nigel Olsson: percussion
Gus Dudgeon: rhino whistle
Jean-Louis Chautemps, Alain Hatot: saxophone
David Hentschel: synthesizer
'Legs' Larry Smith: tap dance
Jacques Bolognesi: trombone
Ivan Julien: trumpet
Recorded: Jan. 1972 at Strawberry Studios, Chateau d'Herouville, France
Producer: Gus Dudgeon
Engineer: Ken Scott
Brass arranger: Gus Dudgeon
Release date: 19 May 1972 (UK), 26 May 1972 (US)
Chart placings: UK: 2, US: 1, CAN: 3, AUS: 15

Sonically, *Honky Chateau* brought Elton's voice front and centre and is where subject matter began to change gear and move away from the familiar country comforts of *Tumbleweed* and *Madman* by broaching contemporary topics and name-checking cultural icons. 'Rocket Man', 'I Think I'm Going to Kill Myself' and 'Amy' were symbolic of this. Some hints of Americana remained in the instrumentation, but the looming dark atmospheres of *Madman Across the Water* were all but gone, replaced by a playfulness which was light on its feet but could have been emphasised even more.

Performances now focused on the core band of Davey, Dee and Nigel, augmented in places by a three-piece horn section and some key appearances by David Hentschel on synthesizer, electric violinist Jean-Luc Ponty and percussionist Ray Cooper.

The venue was Strawberry Studios at the Chateau d'Herouville in France, chosen as a recording location for tax reasons. The one-time home of Polish composer Frédéric Chopin, the Chateau was bought in 1962 by French movie composer Michel Magne. After a fire in 1969, Magne converted it into a residential recording studio.

The entire album was written in four days at the recording sessions, setting the template for future Elton albums. On board as engineer was Ken Scott, renowned for his work with The Beatles, David Bowie and Procol Harum. Extra backing vocalists were used for 'Salvation' and 'Hercules', but a new development saw Davey, Dee and Nigel take control of the backing vocal department, often arranging and recording their parts at night while Elton slept. This was one of many conveniences allowed by living on the estate for the duration of the project. They'd all come down in the morning, have breakfast and then retire to the studio, where Elton would put a new lyric sheet on the piano, write the song in twenty minutes, and then proceed to record. This continued at the rate of about three songs a day. Elton used the smaller upstairs studio which had a more intimate setting, appropriate for recording small bands. The larger downstairs facility was used for orchestral recordings.

Honky Chateau went on to become the first of seven consecutive number one Elton John albums in the USA.

'Honky Cat' (Elton John, Bernie Taupin)
Released as a single A-side, August 1972 (UK), b/w 'Lady Samantha' and 'It's Me That You Need'. UK: 31.
Released as a single A-side, 31 July 1972 (US), b/w 'Slave'. US: 8. CAN: 10. AUS: 31. NZ: 4.
The second single from *Honky Chateau* also acted as album-opener. Where *Madman Across the Water* had opened with someone reaching Los Angeles, here a country boy dreams of kicking up his heels in New Orleans or somewhere like it, in spite of the people at home warning him against it. This desire was matched by the carefree mood of the piano introduction and Davey Johnstone's pumping banjo. Producer Gus Dudgeon's three-piece horn arrangement also gave new life by breathing an untapped dimension into Elton's sound. Add both an acoustic and electric piano, and you got a fairly full instrumental line-up, but with all musical pieces falling into the jigsaw effortlessly.

American country rock band Country Gazette released a glorious bluegrass version of 'Honky Cat' on their 1973 album, *Don't Give Up Your Day Job*. This was quite possibly the finest cover of an Elton number yet.

In light of the first *Honky Chateau* single, 'Rocket Man', reaching number six in the USA and number two in the UK, 'Honky Cat' was a respectable follow-up – its rhythmic tripping of the light fantastic clearly agreeing with record buyers. An Elton John album would not open in such a sprightly and positive manner again until *Caribou*, three albums down the track.

'Mellow' (Elton John, Bernie Taupin)
Back in familiar territory, the loping piano introduction here recalls 'Country Comfort' and 'Amoreena'. With its appropriately mellow funky R&B approach, 'Mellow' in general could have been 'Amoreena - Part Two', but this time with Davey Johnstone's biting wah-wah spicing up the choruses. Like 'Honky Cat' there is more kicking up of the heels, but like 'Amoreena' it is of an erotic nature.

Fresh from German sessions for his *Open Strings* album was French electric violinist Jean-Luc Ponty. His tremolo solo commencing at 3m:25s brought an exotic edge that continued through the later choruses, being raised and reduced in volume where appropriate, to the song's end.

'I Think I'm Going to Kill Myself' (Elton John, Bernie Taupin)

A light-hearted jaunty New Orleans-style look at teenage suicide contemplation. Clearly, it was intended to be taken lightly and used the trick of dark subject over happy music to take the heat off.

With *Honky Chateau*, Davey, Dee and Nigel took on the challenge of arranging and performing backing vocals, in this case adding a smooth and poppy colouring to the half-time post-chorus sections and their further prefacing of the 'Goodbye Yellow Brick Road' intro chord pattern motif. Lightening things up even further was 'Legs' Larry Smith, drummer for the Bonzo Dog Doo-Dah Band, who tap-danced his way through the two closing and virtually instrumental choruses.

Ultimately the track had an uplifting feel reminiscent of the British music hall or, considering the French setting, perhaps even a hint of the Paris Grand Guignol theatre of horror, still fresh in the mind, having only closed its doors ten years prior.

'Susie (Dramas)' (Elton John, Bernie Taupin)

Released as a single B-side, 17 April 1972 (US), b/w 'Rocket Man'.
Similar to 'I Think I'm Going to Kill Myself', 'Susie (Dramas)' softens a semi-dark lyric with a forthright funky rhythm and a harmonic blues overtone. The narrator is happy to be used by his pretty dancer girlfriend, stealing whatever moments he can get with her. He feels he's hit the jackpot despite the fact she's 'living with her funky family in a derelict old alley'.

The star of the show must surely be Davey Johnstone's idiosyncratic guitar solo which stabs its angular way towards the closing choruses, taking subtle and possibly sub-conscious cues from Frank Zappa, Johnny Winter and Dave Edmunds along the way.

'Rocket Man (I Think it's Going to Be a Long Long Time)' (Elton John, Bernie Taupin)

Released as a single A-side, April 1972 (UK), b/w 'Holiday Inn' and 'Goodbye'. UK: 2.
Released as a single A-side, 17 April 1972 (US and CAN), b/w 'Susie (Dramas)'. US: 6. CAN: 8.
Released as a double A-side single, May 1972 (AUS and NZ), b/w 'Tiny Dancer'. AUS: 13. NZ: 11.
If you take a popular cultural symbol, such as an astronaut, turn it into a phrase that pops, such as 'Rocket Man', a title American fiction writer Ray

Bradbury used in his 1951 collection, *The Illustrated Man*, then the battle for its success is half won. There's no denying the power of a title like that – a blueprint that goes straight to the imagination to be instantly turned into a visual. This was the first Elton song title to be that striking. On a night drive, Taupin was struck enough by the appearance in his head of the entire first verse, that he had to constantly repeat the lines to himself so he could write them down upon arriving home.

The appearance of 'Rocket Man' was timely. There was some accusation that the song borrowed from David Bowie's 'Space Oddity', but other than the topic and slow tempo, there is barely any similarity between them. 'Rocket Man' probably bears more similarity to Bread's 1972 hit 'The Guitar Man' than 'Space Oddity' anyway. The suggestion was more than likely fuelled by the fact that the two tracks shared the same producer - Gus Dudgeon. Remember, fate could have been tempted even further, of course, by the presence of engineer Ken Scott, the producer of David Bowie's 'Life On Mars?', so in hindsight 'Rocket Man' was a subtle production considering the producers responsible for the two big pre-existing space songs were both in the room working on this third one.

Bowie's 'Space Oddity' achieved its sense of the universe through a combination of Mellotron, tremolo guitar and, of all things, Stylophone – a children's miniature toy keyboard where notes are played by sliding an attached pencil across the keys. 'Rocket Man' took a more subtle approach by simply utilising slide guitar for a sense of lift-off along with minimal use of ARP synthesizer – an addition which in 1972 instantly shifted any music into the futuristic. Even so, its performance on 'Rocket Man' was limited to some pointed lines in the second verse and subtle accompaniment in the closing section – hardly a science-fiction spectacular.

That year, UK label Pama Records issued a contrasting cover of 'Rocket Man' by reggae band In Flames, showing again that the song could easily survive without the need for electronic embellishment.

The song has remained a staple of the live set to this day, Elton apparently even re-titling it to 'Cosmonaut' as a kind of in-joke on the 1979 Russian concert set-list. But the most elaborate version can be found in the 1986 live concert broadcast from the Sydney Entertainment Centre. The 13-minute extravaganza highlights the superb musicianship of the band which at that time included Johnstone, Olsson and Alan Parsons Project bassist David Paton. Along the way, the performance moves through a kaleidoscope of arrangement touches including brief quotes from Joe Cocker's 'Feelin' Alright' and The Beatles' 'Hey Jude'.

'Salvation' (Elton John, Bernie Taupin)
This slow and unassuming gospel ballad with its lyrical themes of emancipation recalling *Tumbleweed Connection* was Elton's choice for another single at one point. The idea was stated in sixteen scant lines but lacked power

in its delivery. The song was pure, but played very safe and was simply overshadowed by stronger material.

It can be appreciated more on an instrumental level, as it features the worthy augmentation of Davey Johnstone's tasteful guitar volume touches and the interesting ingredient of three simultaneously playing slide guitar solos.

'Slave' (Elton John, Bernie Taupin)

Released as a single B-side, 31 July 1972 (US), b/w 'Honky Cat'.

Even more befitting *Tumbleweed* than 'Salvation', the lyric of this country dirge was from the standpoint of a slave who mentions 'A rumour of a war that's yet to come, That may free our families and our sons'. But the tone was undermined by the unnecessary repetition of the last three syllables of every verse line.

An earlier up-tempo take can be heard on the 1992 *Rare Masters* compilation. The verse syllable repetitions worked well on that more energetic rendition which seemed perfectly suitable for a live show and may well have satisfied the need for that one extra slice of pizzazz that *Honky Chateau* seemed to lack.

'Amy' (Elton John, Bernie Taupin)

It's been said that 'Amy' was a tongue-in-cheek dedication to either Gus Dudgeon's wife Sheila or Bernie's old friend Sally Bennington. There was also later conjecture that Bennington was at least a partial muse for 'Bennie and the Jets' the following year. But there's no doubt the 'Amy' lyric addresses a young man's desire for an older woman who is out of his league.

Instrumentally the song offers a lot. Reminiscent of 'Ballad of a Well-Known Gun', the introduction takes on a more Leon Russell angle with bluesy piano chops against Ray Cooper's sole percussive contribution to the album. A mid-song highlight, Jean-Luc Ponty's searing electric violin solo, perfectly illustrates the frustration involved, but never as intensely as the post-coda closing section where the instrument cries in agonising double-stops.

'Mona Lisas and Mad Hatters' (Elton John, Bernie Taupin)

This colourful ballad takes a more intimate approach. It's like Elton is sitting in front of you singing it. He sings accompanying himself in two-part harmony on the chorus, breaking into three for the word 'night'. Otherwise, the instrumentation is a minimal blend of piano, acoustic guitar, bass and the sparkle of multiple mandolins.

The lyric is accessible, its abstraction more entertaining than alienating. Bernie was shaken by his first impressions of Manhattan. The day they first arrived in 1970, a man had been shot in the street below Bernie's midtown hotel room, which led him to write this lyric. An ode to New York specifically, it could apply to any large city and its struggling anonymous population.

'Hercules' (Elton John, Bernie Taupin)

Like 'Salvation', 'Hercules' was touted as a possible single, this time making it to production but not to release. It is the closest thing to a rock song that the album offers. Almost Bowie-esque in its glorious abstraction, the lyric twists and turns its way through several possible interpretations. Is it the standard cliché of the weakling having sand kicked in his face? Does it refer simply to Elton's legal name change to Elton Hercules John in December 1971, or to his then residence in Virginia Water, Surrey, and its boulder inscribed with the name Hercules at the front gates?

The liner notes for the 1995 CD edition of *Honky Chateau* suggest that the song was actually about a rhinoceros. But in 1984, Elton declared at an Australian concert that the song indeed referred to his name change. Further to this, in a 1974 TV interview on *Russell Harty Plus*, Elton joked that he chose the middle name because the only thing he could think of at the time was Steptoe's horse, Hercules. (*Steptoe and Son* was a BBC 1 sitcom that ran for twelve years to 1974.)

Musically the track is a shuffle that progresses energetically, with a central slide guitar solo from Davey interjected by Gus Dudgeon's Rhino whistle. Choruses are highlighted by Beach Boys-esque backing vocals compliments of Johnstone, Murray and Olsson.

'Hercules' brings *Honky Chateau* to a close on an upbeat high note. Elton would not close an album this way again until *Blue Moves* in 1976.

Don't Shoot Me I'm Only the Piano Player (1973)

Personnel:
Elton John: vocals, pianos, Mellotron, harmonium, organ
Davey Johnstone, Dee Murray, Nigel Olsson: backing vocals
Dee Murray: bass
Nigel Olsson: drums, maracas
Davey Johnstone: guitar, banjo, sitar, mandolin
Jean-Louis Chautemps, Alain Hatot: saxophones
Ken Scott: synthesizer
Jacques Bolognesi: trombone
Ivan Julien: trumpet
Recorded: June/July 1972 at Strawberry Studios, Chateau d'Herouville, France
Producer: Gus Dudgeon
Engineer: Ken Scott
Brass arranger: Gus Dudgeon
Orchestral arranger: Paul Buckmaster
Release date: 26 January 1973 (UK), 22 January 1973 (USA)
Chart placings: UK: 1, US: 1, CAN: 1, AUS: 1

Once again ensconced at the Chateau d'Herouville in France, the songs for *Don't Shoot Me I'm Only the Piano Player* were written in four days and recorded over June and July 1972. Being a transitional record to an extent, the album proved itself by hitting number one in multiple countries and spawning two hit singles in 'Crocodile Rock' and 'Daniel', the former becoming Elton's first American number one, and the latter winning the UK's Ivor Novello songwriting award for 1973. The album became that year's biggest seller in the UK.

In America, MCA swallowed up their subsidiary record labels, including Elton's US label Uni, making *Don't Shoot Me* and the 'Crocodile Rock' single the first releases on the MCA label. Initial pressings were on black labels, followed by the more familiar rainbow design.

There are conflicting stories as to where the album title came from. It's largely believed that at a Hollywood party, Groucho Marx teased Elton that his name was around the wrong way and was actually John Elton. Elton replied, 'Don't shoot me, I'm only the piano player.' However, Bernie Taupin at one stage claimed the title came from a plaque he found in an American junk shop.

'Daniel' (Elton John, Bernie Taupin)

Released as a single A-side, January 1973 (UK), 26 March 1973 (US), b/w 'Skyline Pigeon'. UK: 4. US: 2. CAN: 1. AUS: 7. NZ: 2.

In the 1991 *Two Rooms: Celebrating the Songs of Elton John and Bernie Taupin* liner notes, Bernie said 'Daniel' was inspired by a *Newsweek* article about Vietnam veterans. It's been the most misinterpreted song of their career, apparently due to Elton omitting a final verse that explained the story, a verse that Bernie has denied existed.

This editing of lyrics on Elton's part was not uncommon, also happening with 'Candle in the Wind' and 'Bennie and the Jets'. In a 1997 *Billboard Magazine* interview, Bernie stated that he often wrote middle eight (or bridge) sections that Elton would omit. There is a story that Davey Johnstone once told Gus Dudgeon that the missing 'Daniel' verse included a line about 'a ship's dog named Paul'. In the interview, Bernie said that sounded unlikely, adding he had no memory of the verse. Johnstone claimed the verse was so out of character with the rest of the song that Elton tore it from the page, discarding it on the very day he wrote the music.

No real harm was done. The song not only hit the top ten in multiple countries and number one in Canada, but it won the prestigious Ivor Novello award for 1973 and earned Elton the Grammy for Best Male Pop Vocal Performance the following year. To top it off, the recording was used in Martin Scorsese's successful 1974 movie, *Alice Doesn't Live Here Anymore*.

Surprisingly, cover versions failed to pour from the studios. But of note was Ivan 'Boogaloo Joe' Jones' 1973 Latin jazz guitar rendition, followed in 1974 by The Jimmy Castor Bunch featuring The Everything Man, who gifted a saxophone-led instrumental embracing the new disco craze on their hilariously-titled album, *Butt Of Course*.

Easily Elton's most MOR track since 'Friends' thanks to the combination of acoustic guitar and Fender Rhodes electric piano, the agreeable noise that was 'Daniel' was beautifully adorned by engineer Ken Scott's modernising synthesizer solo, providing the technological stepping-stone from 'Rocket Man' to the coming 'Funeral for a Friend'.

'Teacher I Need You' (Elton John, Bernie Taupin)

Released as a single A-side, 31 March 1973 (NOR), b/w 'High Flying Bird'.
The more rousing second track was inspired by a bygone golden age of pop, but demonstrated that less extravagantly than its album-mate, 'Crocodile Rock'. Elton has said that with 'Teacher I Need You' he was thinking, at least vocally, of every Bobby Vee record he'd ever heard.

This exposition of a pupil's crush on his teacher was play-listed on album-oriented rock radio stations in the USA. Here in New Zealand at the time we only had non-formatted eclectic AM pop/rock stations, so some album cuts, including this one, were treated as singles and put in general rotation, though of course they never charted. The song was, however, released as a single in Norway in 1973. It's pop accessibility was undeniable but nicely offset by the drama of backwards-reverb piano flourishes that appeared in the introduction and its repetitions throughout.

'Elderberry Wine' (Elton John, Bernie Taupin)

Released as a single B-side, 27 October 1972 (UK), 20 November 1972 (US), b/w 'Crocodile Rock'.
The B-side of 'Crocodile Rock', issued three months in advance of the album in

the UK, acted as an enticing teaser for what was to come. The A-side was one thing, but the real juice was in this B-side (excuse the pun). At that stage the single buyer wouldn't have known if this was for album inclusion or not, so it would have been a real find for a fan.

The narrator hasn't seen his wife for a year and is living in a funk, dreaming of when they'd once shared the domestic moonshine that could be bought off the shelf. The instantly accessible song used the recipe of slightly-down lyric over upbeat and joyous music. It also got generous radio-play, thereby making the single a kind of double A-side.

'Blues for Baby and Me' (Elton John, Bernie Taupin)

Track four signalled the return of arranger Paul Buckmaster, whose subtle strings gave some hope to a difficult lyric. If there was ever a sitter for a hit cover recording, it was this song. Perhaps a bit dark for an Elton single, I'm amazed no one else took it on at the time and made it into the hit it could have been. I can only put it down to the first verse lyric where the narrator wants to take his girl west, away from her father who says, 'He'll get you in trouble, I know it, Those bums are all the same'. Maybe not single fodder, but the lines could have come out as completely benign in the hands of an appropriate artist such as James Taylor.

It's a beautiful ballad that reflects its time, with a lyric that seeps a youthful naivete – not in composition but in theme. Davey Johnstone's sitar lines hark a few years back to a carefree psychedelic time that was all but gone by 1973, compounding the lyric's realities of life and their bad habit of hanging around. That's the vibe this recording captures – a snapshot of a cultural crossroads.

'Midnight Creeper' (Elton John, Bernie Taupin)

The slightly undesirable hero here unforgivingly wears his failings on his sleeve. He believes those long-haired ladies locked in his cellar full of cheap red wine, don't really mind. Is 'Blues for Baby and Me' sounding more like a single *now?*

The lyric might be dark, but appealing musical qualities are obvious; a stonkin' brass arrangement courtesy of Gus Dudgeon, and not one but two idiosyncratic guitar solos from Davey Johnstone, not to mention those Pete Townshend-esque accented guitar flourishes that greatly enhance the choruses.

A nod to the Rolling Stones in a kind of rock/soul hybrid, 'Midnight Creeper' is indeed a creeper, but not as creepy in effect as the next song.

'Have Mercy on the Criminal' (Elton John, Bernie Taupin)

Buckmaster strikes! Returning temporarily to the orchestral glories of *Madman Across the Water*, but this time the string section colours a background reminiscent of The Beatles' 'I Want You (She's So Heavy)', landmarked by Derek and the Dominos' 'Layla' if the repeating guitar riff is anything to go by. Those notes are the same as 'Layla' but in a lower key and delayed in time by one beat. However, the lick is developed, finding its most extended incarnation at the end.

The entire mood is dark. No downer lyric on top of happy music here. An escaped prisoner is on the lam; his predicament relayed to us in the third-person. But it ends up in the second verse that the narrator may be speaking of his own past experience.

The shrill tone of Davey Johnstone's guitar solo pierces the darkness, at first doubled, then tripled an octave down, dialling up the pressure with a vibe that would be perfected on *Goodbye Yellow Brick Road* – an album that could have easily housed 'Have Mercy On the Criminal'.

It's a swansong of a sort, at least for a while where Paul Buckmaster was concerned. This track was the end of an era in a way. Though his work with Elton was not yet done, Buckmaster would never darken Elton's musical door in quite the same way again.

'I'm Gonna Be a Teenage Idol' (Elton John, Bernie Taupin)

By this stage, Elton was fast becoming a teenage idol himself, but rather than proving to be prophetic, this lyric was, in fact, dedicated to pop star Marc Bolan. Elton even sounded exactly, perhaps purposefully, like Bolan on the chorus lyric line 'Just give me a break'. According to a 1997 *Billboard Magazine* interview with Elton, when he played the song for Bolan, he was seemingly unmoved, showing no reaction whatsoever.

The character in the song is desperate for fame, drinking himself to sleep at night, praying to the teenage god of rock to make him 'A motivated supersonic king of the scene'. Potential hit single fodder maybe, but the story had a dark tone, and the slow funk was likely considered un-danceable at the time. A single of this could well have ended up being the disc they slip on as everyone's leaving the disco. Not ideal.

But something about this track gets under the skin still. It might be the stabbing horns. Or it might be those acoustic guitars that really kick on the word 'motivated' every time. These were the days when moments like that on a record could keep you on cloud nine for weeks.

'Texan Love Song' (Elton John, Bernie Taupin)

Of the *Don't Shoot Me* album cuts that were given regular radio-play here in New Zealand, 'Texan Love Song' got the most. It deserved to be a single, but this threatening campfire sing-along all but swore and may have been perceived as a novelty by some, securing a level of ongoing popularity. The lack of piano skewed the formula too, making the song not immediately obvious as an Elton track.

Brought into the present by an updated vernacular, the song prolonged the Americana aspect, a carrot that would occasionally be dangled for a few years yet. To quote the lyric, 'Goddammit', it was also as hooky as hell and stuck in your brain, just like all good radio songs should. The built-in hooks overshadowed any negative connotations, which in my book makes 'Texan Love Song' a semi-country classic, with a melody that sounds like it's been around forever, just like Bernie's original country inspiration, the Marty Robbins classic, 'El Paso'.

'Crocodile Rock' (Elton John, Bernie Taupin)

Released as a single A-side, 27 October 1972 (UK), 20 November 1972 (US), b/w 'Elderberry Wine'. UK: 5. USA: 1. CAN: 1. AUS: 2. NZ: 1.

The first MCA single, 'Crocodile Rock' – or, as it was lovingly translated in Mexico, 'El Rock Del Cocodrilo' – soared like a large winged lizard to the top of the charts in the US and Canada. Elton's first US number one single, it wore its American rock and roll heritage proudly through the use of the 'Speedy Gonzales' la-la motif by way of a standard doo-wop chord progression.

Elton made no secret that the recording was derivative, additionally taking inspiration from Australian band Daddy Cool's hit 'Eagle Rock' after hearing it on a recent trip down under. But in 1974, a lawsuit was filed in Los Angeles on behalf of 'Speedy Gonzales' part-author, Buddy Kaye, laughably citing 'illegally incorporated chords which produced a falsetto tone'. These, of course, were chords which had previously been incorporated into a thousand doo-wop songs, much like thousands of blues songs all share the same progression, which is partially what makes them blues in the first place.

The matter was, ultimately, dismissed and settled out of court. But it's understandable how it could have become an issue. Retrospective musical styling was a relatively new thing, at least in the pop charts. Frank Zappa's 1968 album *Cruising with Ruben and the Jets* had been an absolute tribute to '50s rock and roll and doo-wop but went largely unnoticed by all except the cadre of his hardcore audience. But in 1973, 'Crocodile Rock' was in the ear of everyone, whether they wanted it there or not. Whether it was taken seriously or not, it set a precedent for the public at large and paved a way, making the road easier for upcoming retro-focused hits like Wizzard's future UK number one 'See My Baby Jive', which was only six months away.

'Crocodile Rock' settled on number 5 in the UK. As for 'El Rock Del Cocodrilo', it featured both 'Elderberry Wine' and 'High Flying Bird' on its B-side, translated as 'Vino De Elderberry', and the gorgeous-sounding 'Pajaro Volador'.

'High Flying Bird' (Elton John, Bernie Taupin)

Being a reasonably happy ballad, 'High Flying Bird' could have made a good single. But minus the energy of 'Crocodile Rock' or 'Elderberry Wine' and lacking the emotional power of 'Blues for Baby and Me', it functioned perfectly as a closer.

There was a hint of the afore-mentioned Mick Jagger vocal twang in places, though Elton has said he was thinking more of Van Morrison here. The band's shining backing vocals elevated the choruses and coda, bringing to a satisfying close, an album that can be thought of as a transition between the skin-shedding of *Honky Chateau* and the indefinable presence that was etched into every bar of the coming *Goodbye Yellow Brick Road*.

Contemporary Tracks:
'Skyline Pigeon' (Elton John, Bernie Taupin)
Released as a single B-side, January 1973 (UK), 26 March 1973 (US), b/w 'Skyline Pigeon'.

'Skyline Pigeon' was developed into a more fleshed-out and definitive full band arrangement for this re-recording from the *Don't Shoot Me* sessions. As the B-side of 'Daniel', it shared in that song's success and even earned a third recording at the 1974 Royal Festival Hall concert, part of which was released on the 1976 *Here and There* live album.

Goodbye Yellow Brick Road (1973)

Personnel:
Elton John: vocals, pianos, Mellotron, organ
Kiki Dee, Davey Johnstone, Dee Murray, Nigel Olsson: backing vocals
Dee Murray: bass
Nigel Olsson: drums, congas, tambourine
Davey Johnstone: guitars, pedal steel, banjo
Ray Cooper: percussion
Leroy Gomez: saxophone
David Hentschel: synthesizer
Prince Rhino: vocal interjections
Recorded: May 1973 at Strawberry Studios, Chateau d'Herouville, France, Trident Studios, London
Producer: Gus Dudgeon
Engineer: David Hentschel
Orchestral arranger: Del Newman
Release date: 5 October 1973 (UK), 5 October 1973 (US)
Chart placings: UK: 1, US: 1, CAN: 1, AUS: 1

For three days in January 1973, Elton locked himself in a room at the Pink Flamingo hotel in Kingston, Jamaica, to write the majority of the songs which were to form *Goodbye Yellow Brick Road*. He has since claimed, in jest, that he had no choice but to write since he was too scared to leave the hotel due to the nature of inner Kingston, which was experiencing local unrest due to economic depression. Some comfort came in the form of American jazz pianist Les McCann, who was playing in the hotel courtyard.

Jamaica was considered as a location after the Rolling Stones recorded much of *Goat's Head Soup* there at Dynamic Sound. Elton and band arrived in town to chaos on the day after the Joe Frazier/George Foreman fight. To make matters worse, men carrying machine guns hung around on the street, and the studio was surrounded by barbed wire. People rocked the band's mini-bus as it arrived. To get to the studio, the band had to run the gauntlet of striking picketers outside who blew crushed fibres at them through blowpipes, which resulted in a skin rash for some. The whole environment was described by Ken Scott, who accompanied them on the trip, as being like New Year's Eve in Times Square lasting for a week.

Unfortunately, the studio piano was deemed by Elton to be woefully inadequate and, discussing the need for microphones, the studio owner yelled 'Carlton, get the microphone!' Used to using upwards of a dozen microphones on the drums alone, at this point the band knew they were in deep trouble.

A recording of 'Saturday Night's Alright for Fighting' was attempted, but the playback sounded like a transistor radio, after which the band panicked. Equipment was promised, but days passed, and it never arrived. Eventually, deciding to leave Jamaica, the final exit from Kingston became a scramble to the airport. Dee Murray later recalled running for the nearest vehicle on the day; it was that dramatic. Elton and Bernie endured a frantic taxi ride cutting across sugar cane fields to the airport. Adding insult to injury, the band equipment was impounded.

In May 1973, after an extensive British tour, the band reconvened in France, grateful to be recording in the familiar surroundings of the Chateau d'Herouville. Some songs were still to be written, Elton attending to this daily over breakfast as the others ate. They would then have a quick acoustic run-through of the just-written song or songs in the breakfast room, then head to the studio to record them at the rate of from one to four a day.

Feeling he'd been writing about American culture too much, Bernie now incorporated cinematic themes and trans-Atlantic portraits of sincere and decadent characters, real and imagined, in happy and hopeless situations. The scenery was again often overcast, despite the sunny album cover illustration showing Elton stepping into a poster onto a yellow brick road - a road which actually existed, not in the promised land, but in England.

Intended as a single album, enough worthy material appeared to guarantee a substantial double. With Ken Scott unavailable as engineer, his replacement was Trident's David Hentschel. The recording was completed in eighteen days. Even as the album was being mixed back in London at Trident, working album titles still included *Vodka and Tonics* and *Silent Movies, Talking Pictures*. This is where the orchestra was added, arrangements this time by Del Newman who had orchestrated Wings' James Bond movie theme, 'Live and Let Die', the previous October. Additional overdubs at this stage were some guitar parts, percussion, and David Hentschel's synthesizer introduction to 'Funeral for a Friend'.

All of the above paid off with what became the *Goodbye Yellow Brick Road* album hitting number one in multiple countries and achieving the USA's number one album of the year for 1974.

'Funeral for a Friend' (Elton John)

The introduction to 'Funeral for a Friend' was the last thing recorded for the album. Gus Dudgeon originally wanted to use the 20th Century Fox overture but couldn't get clearance, so he suggested to engineer and musician David Hentschel that he come up with an arrangement to act as an overture that could segue into 'Funeral for a Friend' itself. The idea was to find melodies and chord sequences from the album's songs that could easily run together to make a flowing composition.

The band section for 'Funeral for a Friend' itself was recorded along with 'Candle in the Wind' and 'Bennie and the Jets' on the first recording day of Monday 7 May 1973. Going forward a few weeks to Trident Studios in London, David Hentschel arranged the introductory section up to where the piano enters, incorporating themes from 'I've Seen That Movie Too', 'The Ballad of Danny Bailey', 'Candle in the Wind' and some others, performing it on an ARP

2500 synthesizer. The upper keyboard was capable of playing two notes at a time, but doing that, things became imprecise with the keyboard becoming volatile, so each voice was played monophonically. Hentschel spent three or four days writing the arrangement and then recorded it at Trident in a day. According to Davey Johnstone, upon hearing the completed piece, the band were initially unsure. But on the second playing, it hit them how great it was and how well it was going to work.

The evocative piece has been described as Wagnerian and an example of the progressive rock that was prevalent at the time. True or not, it possessed a definite X factor deeming it, along with its partner 'Love Lies Bleeding', as worthy of extensive airplay on album-oriented rock stations in the USA. It also earned a not-too-shabby easy-listening cover version by the Simon Park Orchestra on their 1974 album, *Something in the Air*.

'Love Lies Bleeding' (Elton John, Bernie Taupin)

Bernie Taupin has claimed in the past to have no memory of writing this, but he did confirm in a contemporary interview that the lyric was related to show business and its rigours wrought on marriage.

The vocals were finely performed with a bite and extended vocal range that Elton continued to show throughout the album. More monophonic synth layering as rendered in 'Funeral for a Friend' occurred fading slowly into the suspenseful instrumental mid-section with its eerie staccato Mellotron chords. Davey Johnstone's howling guitar solo followed, its voice continuing on to intensify throughout the closing instrumental section, a rock workout the like of which we hadn't heard since the finale of 'Burn Down the Mission'.

The song attracted a 1975 cover version by French singer Richard Anthony in a fair lower-key replica translated as 'L'amour Se Meurt Entre Mes Mains'.

'Funeral for a Friend' and 'Love Lies Bleeding' combined to make a respectable album opener indeed, and certainly one appropriate for a double. Elton would do exactly the opposite on his next double album, 1976's *Blue Moves*, opening with a miniature instrumental composition he didn't even write and barely played on, if at all.

'Candle in the Wind' (Elton John, Bernie Taupin)

Released as a single A-side, February 1974 (UK, AUS and NZ), b/w 'Bennie and the Jets'. UK: 11. AUS: 5. NZ: 5.
Released as a single B-side, 1974 (DEN), b/w 'Jamaica Jerk-Off'.'
In a 2011 *Sound on Sound* magazine interview, David Hentschel recalled witnessing Elton writing 'Candle in the Wind'. Hentschel came down for breakfast one morning at the Chateau and as he and the others ate, Elton sat in the corner at the dining room piano and wrote the song from the lyric Bernie had handed him the night before. After a quick acoustic run-through in the dining room, they recorded the song an hour later, and that was that. In recording, the ideas would always flow naturally. In this case, Elton

suggested the guitar lick for Davey Johnstone to play at the end of the chorus. Unconvinced at first, Johnstone tried it and it worked.

Three or four songs were written that way on this album, the majority of the material having been written in Jamaica. Bernie has spoken of virtual automatic writing in a kind of stream-of-consciousness, which was borne out by the lines, 'While those around you crawled, They crawled out of the woodwork' and 'Loneliness was tough, The toughest role you ever played'.

At the time Elton and Bernie both claimed that the other was the Marilyn Monroe fanatic, Elton admitting to being fascinated by her or any similar show business icon such as Mae West or Marlene Dietrich. Bernie claimed the song could just as easily have been about James Dean or Jim Morrison. The point was to express an idea about the price of fame and how death is glamourised, making stars immortal. He used Marilyn as a metaphor for how the industry could misuse stars.

Backed with 'Bennie and the Jets', the 'Candle in the Wind' single was a practical double A-side. But it was not Released as a single in the USA.

Of special mention is the thoroughly avant-garde 1975 cover version by Australian singer Julie Anthony, that sounded like a new age version of the Mothers of Invention meeting Joni Mitchell.

'Bennie and the Jets' (Elton John, Bernie Taupin)

Released as a single B-side, February 1974 (UK, AUS and NZ), b/w 'Candle in the Wind'. UK: 37. AUS: 5. NZ: 5.
Released as a single A-side, 4 February 1974 (US and CAN), b/w 'Harmony'. US: 1. CAN: 1.
Released as a single A-side, 9 September 1976 (UK), b/w 'Rock and Roll Madonna'. UK: 37.

After being cut on the first recording day at the Chateau, along with the rest of what became side one, 'Bennie and the Jets' underwent a transformation back at Trident during the mixing process. David Hentschel noticed Elton had struck a chord at the very beginning exactly four beats before the band started. Hentschel thought it sounded like somebody on stage trying to cue a band to start. He threw a slap echo on everything and flew in onto the tape some applause from Jimi Hendrix live at the Isle of Wight and Elton live at the Royal Festival Hall. Gus, David and assistant Peter Kelsey then recorded themselves clapping, stomping and whistling through the song. A delay unit was then used to multiply the track to sound like a concert hall full of people. Elton wasn't told they'd done it, but on first hearing the final mix, he loved it.

Initially, the song was viewed as an oddity by all involved. Bernie said it was supposed to be about a prototypical science fiction female rock and roll band, but referred to it as a throwaway nevertheless. Everyone eventually warmed to it, but Elton doubted its commercial appeal and fought against MCA issuing the song as a single in America. But learning it had hit number one on the black airplay chart in Detroit, he relented, after which it was released, reaching number one in both the USA and Canada. The single reaching number fifteen on the *Billboard Hot Soul Singles* chart led to Elton performing the hit on a May 1975 episode of the black music TV show, *Soul Train*. This led to the enduring myth that he was the first white performer on the show ever.

'Bennie and the Jets' was eventually issued as an A-side single in the UK in September 1976, but it stalled at number 37, eclipsed by the ongoing spate of Elton releases, including the recent number one duet with Kiki Dee, 'Don't Go Breaking My Heart'.

'Goodbye Yellow Brick Road' (Elton John, Bernie Taupin)
Released as a single A-side, 7 September 1973 (UK), 15 October 1973 (US) b/w 'Screw You' (Re-titled 'Young Man's Blues' (US)). UK: 6. US: 2. CAN: 1. AUS: 4. NZ: 1.

Stating the five-chord sequence first found in 'Son of Your Father' once-and-for-all as a major theme, the album's title track and second single lyrically unveiled the desire for an escape hatch from the pressures of success. There was much speculation as to the lyric's layered metaphors, which only served to confuse the budding interpreter.

But one interesting fact seems to have had a bearing on the cloudy origins of this popular number. In the early '70s, Bernie and Maxine purchased a home on Beck Hill in the village of Tealby, Lincolnshire, half a mile from where there once stood a vast 1800s Gothic mansion named Bayons Manor. The mansion had been built on the location of an older house once owned by the brother of William the Conqueror. Sadly, Bayons Manor became derelict over time, being demolished in 1964, leaving nothing but ruins. But the final touch the then-current owner made was to take the yellow Lincolnshire stone the mansion was built from and use it to pave a road that circled the quarter-of-a-mile wide estate. This was a ten-minute walk from Bernie's home at the other end of Beck Hill road, to which Elton was a known visitor as there would sometimes be a fuss from his Rolls Royce blocking the narrow street, so he would most likely also have been aware of the nearby exotic location.

The lyric does refer to the road from *The Wizard of Oz* as a metaphor for success, but also to the road back home, mixed in with other grand and small references to create the esoteric lyrical brew that Bernie was so adept at stirring. He described the song in a *Sound on Sound* magazine interview as possibly being about the all-encompassing world of fame and whether it's really everything it's cracked up to be. He also spoke of the song's search for a happy medium and a way to exist as successful in a tranquil setting.

The vocal was recorded late one night after midnight, and as the song neared its end, saxophonist Leroy Gomez and friends walked up the outer stairs behind the studio just in time to hear Elton sing the closing lines that would end up on the recording. The moment it was finished, and the recording light went out, the door at the top of the back studio stairs opened to reveal Gomez and friends. Hearing a sax player was needed, but there had as yet been little luck in finding the right one, Leroy's friends had bundled him up and dragged him down to the studio. He was one of the most sought-after session players in Paris, but even so, the thought of turning up uninvited to an Elton session filled him with horror. Elton and the band were gracious, changed their plans for the session on the spot and recorded Gomez's saxophone on 'Social Disease' and 'Screw You' before the night was out. The gamble had been a success.

Successful too was the single – top ten in multiple countries and number one in Canada and New Zealand. In the USA the song experienced the push/pull of being number two on the official *Billboard* chart and number one in *Cashbox*.

'This Song Has No Title' (Elton John, Bernie Taupin)
From the perspective of an inquisitive beginner, this lyric communicates the desire to write and experience all that the pursuit of any art can bring, as granted by the intangible powers-that-be. Adventurous stuff. But it all unfolds over a rolling 2m:23s of piano, Mellotron and synthesizer, punctuated by a variety of vocal hooks - Elton flawlessly singing in three-part harmony with himself on the choruses. Not often has such an intellectual concept been so inviting and singable. Elton and Bernie's reputation as songwriters of note could have been forged by the existence of this one timeless piece alone.

'Grey Seal' (Elton John, Bernie Taupin)
More than deserving of a second chance at life, the powerfully dynamic re-recording of 'Grey Seal' was a production triumph. The mix alone for its clarity and delineation between instruments stands up against anything you'd hear today.

Elton has described the lyric as surreal. Bernie has called it meaningless. But like 'This Song Has No Title', it conveys a quest for knowledge and could even be perceived as a continuation of that lyric placed as it is in the sequence.

Credit must be given to Neil Barrett of the *I Guess That's Why They Call It the Elton John Podcast* podcast for his research and ultimate theory on the meaning of this enigmatic lyric. He believes some inspiration was planted by the ancient allegory of Plato's Cave. Socrates described a group of prisoners chained to a cave wall their entire lives, their only experience of reality coming from the shadows cast on the opposite wall from objects passing in front of a fire behind them. Not realising they were prisoners at all, but eventually escaping, they then realised there was much more to life.

'Jamaica Jerk-Off' (Elton John, Bernie Taupin)
Released as a single A-side, 1974 (DEN), b/w 'Candle in the Wind'.
Appearing a little off-kilter with the rest of the album, the fun, fast, quirky and potentially commercial 'Jamaica Jerk-Off' is another track that Bernie once claimed to have no memory of writing, accepting that it was probably inspired by the recent trip to Jamaica. That could have been what qualified it for album

inclusion as it was a part of the story. But what qualified it for A-side release only in Denmark, with 'Candle in the Wind' on the flipside, is something that might have to remain a mystery. The same single in Brazil had the A and B sides flipped.

The recording is of historic interest as an early example of a recorded drum unit, though it wasn't the first, beaten by Robin Gibb's 1969 single 'Saved by the Bell' and Sly and the Family Stone's 1971 album, *There's A Riot Goin' On*.

The song received extra attention through a 1974 reggae cover version by The Pioneers, and in 1977 when covered most respectably by British reggae artist, Judge Dread.

'I've Seen That Movie Too' (Elton John, Bernie Taupin)

This dark ballad could have been swapped with 'Jamaica Jerk-Off' in the sequence, so disc one ended on an up note, but as an album, *Goodbye Yellow Brick Road* mostly played to a specific audience and by default a general one. Elton and the crew could do as they pleased by this point, so to end an album side on an intense ballad with dark overtones that may not inspire a casual listener to continue on to side three, was a privilege.

The main character here has the romantic wool pulled over his eyes but has a surprisingly philosophical and rose-tinted attitude toward the game-playing he's become the victim of. The star-twinkler is caught like a deer in his headlights. The game is up, and the argument is made eloquently indeed. But then, that's what the best songs do. The movies here act as an allegory to the lie the narrator exposes. More adventurous stuff, but it works.

Davey's psychedelic guitar solo reflects the situation perfectly, backwards and indistinct in the first half, forwards and resolute in the second, peaking with a combination of both in seagull-like screams mocking the charade. We don't find out what ultimately happens to these two, but under-riding it all is a sadness that pretty much reveals the inevitable.

It's been said that ballads are easy to write, but great ones are difficult to write. In this case, Elton found it easy to write a great one that is close to, if not his finest. 'Candle in the Wind' is in the same ballpark, and the later 'Sorry Seems to Be the Hardest Word' probably equals it in intensity while falling too far over into the saccharine. But 'I've Seen That Movie Too' is an example of a slow-burning love song with its sentimentality under strict control, thanks to a resigned lyric with a realistic outlook.

'Sweet Painted Lady' (Elton John, Bernie Taupin)

Listening on compact disc, minus the benefit of changing record sides enabling a break, the similarly slow 'Sweet Painted Lady' suffers in the shadow of the song before it. Lightened by a shuffle rhythm and a continental air, the soft metaphor of the title is plainly transparent, the narrator sympathising with the ladies of the night. Yes, my metaphor is trite, but it is in keeping with the unfair reception the song received from those who were flummoxed by the lyric's blunt frankness. 'Sweet Painted Lady' probably didn't get a fair crack of the whip for that reason, but its confronting lyric affirmed its belonging amongst the difficult characters living on the edge within the confines of these songs.

Having said that, the plaintive ballad is probably better appreciated out of context, being as it was unfairly sandwiched between its immense fore-runner and superior follower, 'The Ballad of Danny Bailey'. I'd suggest that beginning side three instead with that song followed by 'Sweet Painted Lady' might have made more sense, but the opening line 'I'm back on dry land once again' would certainly have been hard to resist as a re-entry opener to the second disc.

'The Ballad of Danny Bailey (1909-34)' (Elton John, Bernie Taupin)

In *Rolling Stone* magazine, Bernie Taupin revealed how 'The Ballad of Danny Bailey', like 'Rocket Man', was one of those lyrics that sprung from finding the opening lines. 'Some punk with a shotgun killed young Danny Bailey, In cold blood in the lobby of a downtown motel'. From there it became a eulogy to a bootlegger of the gangster era.

The mood is established ominously through the deathly low piano motif and is then built upon by Del Newman's orchestration. Subtle for the most part, the strings eventually slide into the closing instrumental section which builds to an eventual frenzy worthy of the best moves arranger Paul Buckmaster ever offered Elton's material.

This dark piece is a landmark that has passed the test of time and is partially responsible for the continued solid reputation of an album that has come to be regarded as Elton John's '*Sgt. Pepper*'.

'Dirty Little Girl' (Elton John, Bernie Taupin)

Elton never made a secret of his admiration for the Rolling Stones, and if he ever had a song they could have covered, this was it. The loose, slimy groove and bold lyric could have worked on their 1976 opus, *Black and Blue*. In the '70s, songs were safer from censor scrutiny than today, especially in parts of continental Europe. Some radio hits even slipped questionable language through thanks to a lack of clarity on the singer's part, which was probably the point at times. Had it been a single, 'Dirty Little Girl' could have been pulled up for the prominence of the laughably benign word 'bitch' in the choruses - a test that would have meant little to the Rolling Stones, if their 1973 Swiss top ten hit 'Star Star' was anything to go by.

But the swampy groove that was 'Dirty Little Girl' was never a single and stands as another nugget of side three grit keeping this alternately soft and edgy album alive.

'All the Girls Love Alice' (Elton John, Bernie Taupin)

Passing through Elton's compositional filter, there were times when a lyric could undergo transformations to some extent. He might repeat something to create a hook or omit a line or two, or an entire verse, as we've seen. But he was clever enough to clock the definitive character of 'All the Girls Love Alice' for the specific genetic fingerprint it possessed and boldly leave it exactly as presented to him – that is, the tale of a teenage lesbian with a death-wish. To make the song a ballad might have been overly sympathetic, but to make it an out-'n'-out rocker was the magic ingredient that brought the story to life.

To object to the overall subject matter and not write the song at all would have been a choice, but to proceed to write the song and then remove the mysterious death from the story would have been structural blasphemy. Furthermore, to mess with the obvious Beatles lyric reference would have been to close a blind in an already dark room and interfere with the intrinsic power that characterised this entire collection.

In The Beatles' 'I Saw Her Standing There', Paul McCartney began with, 'Well she was just seventeen, You know what I mean'. In the second verse of 'All the Girls Love Alice', Bernie Taupin wrote, 'But what do you expect from a chick who's just sixteen? And hey, hey, hey, you know what I mean'. Quite possibly subconscious, it was a definite tip of the hat to a Beatles lyric that had been considered fairly raunchy itself, at least for 1963 when it appeared.

Davey Johnstone's axe-like chordal guitar stabs set the tone in the rock verses, but the choruses jettisoned the drums, dropping back to piano, prickly synthesizer lines, and backing vocals. Elton's vocal harmonies were here combined with those of British singer Kiki Dee, on the verge of chart success herself after recently signing to Elton's newly-formed label, Rocket Records.

The final re-entry of the drums supported more rock guitar in the form of a solo and flanged string slides, adding to the street-siren cacophony that closed out both the song and the unapologetic spinning circular saw that was side three.

'Your Sister Can't Twist (But She Can Rock 'n' Roll)' (Elton John, Bernie Taupin)

Giving a break from the casualties of side three, side four opened with a frantic rock and roll number you could think of as an even more '50s-sounding 'Crocodile Rock'. Throw in some Beach Boys-like vocal references and what sounded like a Mellotron on a vocal 'aah' sound, and you got a pretty nifty '50s curio that could well have influenced the coming trend of British rock and roll retro bands like Mud and Showaddywaddy.

'Saturday Night's Alright for Fighting' (Elton John, Bernie Taupin)

Released as a single A-side, 29 June 1973 (UK), 16 July 1973 (US) b/w 'Jack Rabbit' and 'Whenever You're Ready (We'll Go Steady Again)'. UK: 7. US: 12. CAN: 12. AUS: 31. NZ: 20.

Feeling that his exploration of Americana had run its course, Bernie attempted to write a lyric that was totally English in nature. The song has often been said to refer to a Lincolnshire pub he would visit when younger, but he claimed that was not necessarily true and was just another example of his lyrics being misinterpreted.

First recorded in the failed and lost Kingston version, 'Saturday Night's Alright for Fighting' found its true voice when re-recorded at the Chateau. But the process wasn't without difficulty. Somehow Elton couldn't get his piano part to sit against the band, resulting in it being the only piano track on the album overdubbed separately from the other performances. Legend has it, too, that in a fit of apparent Jim Morrison inspiration, Elton re-sung the song lying on the floor.

The guitar-dominated rocker issued as the album's first single has remained a popular staple of the live set to this day.

'Roy Rogers' (Elton John, Bernie Taupin)

In contrast to 'Goodbye Yellow Brick Road' which yearned for a post-success levelling-out, the country waltz 'Roy Rogers' ached for an escape from the repetitive workaday routine in exchange for a good night in front of the TV. This ode to the memory of an idolised Hollywood superstar nicely complimented the cinematic references that preceded it and could have made an effective close to the album.

'Social Disease' (Elton John, Bernie Taupin)

Elton has said that the first song written for an album is often a throwaway, which along with the plainly self-lambasting lyric could explain the penultimate position of 'Social Disease' in the album sequence. But I'd defend the song for sounding at worst like a *Honky Chateau* leftover, which isn't bad at all, and at best like a respectable Leon Russell tribute.

An added bonus was the presence of American saxophonist and vocalist, Leroy Gomez, who provided the unobtrusive sax solo which made its point quickly and then was gone - much like his sudden unexpected appearance at the session, the night 'Goodbye Yellow Brick Road' was recorded. In 1977, Leroy Gomez would go on to sing lead on the successful Santa Esmeralda cover of The Animals' '60s hit, 'Don't Let Me Be Misunderstood'.

'Harmony' (Elton John, Bernie Taupin)

Released as a single B-side, 4 February 1974 (US), b/w 'Bennie and the Jets'.
Released as a single B-side, 12 March 1976 (UK), b/w 'Pinball Wizard'.
If someone recommended ending the album on a positive note, Elton listened. Coming in under three minutes, this moody piece encapsulated the overall feeling of the album but topped it off with a happy lyric and closed on an unmistakable major chord.

Slated as a possible fourth single, this idea was mooted due to the advancing scheduled arrival of the new album, *Caribou*, and its first single, 'Don't Let the

An iconic image from a photo shoot at home in 1974. (*Terry O'Neill*)

Left: Original *Empty Sky* 1969 cover artwork by David Larkham. *(Rocket)*

Right: The 1975 US cover for *Empty Sky* with new illustration by Belgian artist Jean Michel Folon. *(Rocket)*

Left: David Larkham's suitably moody cover for the *Elton John* album.

Right: The *Tumbleweed Connection* cover with image shot by David Larkham at Horsted Keynes railway station in Sussex, England, 1970. *(Rocket)*

Left: Cover image for the *Friends* soundtrack, 1971.

Below: The opening titles to the *Friends* movie, 1971.

Above: In this much-seen clip, Elton plays 'Tiny Dancer' on *the Old Grey Whistle Test*, BBC 1971, then presented by Richard Williams. *(BBC)*

Below: TV presenter and producer Humphrey Burton presents an Elton John special on his *Aquarius* Programme on ITV in 1971. *(ITV)*

Above: In concert on BBC TV in 1970 - the show was called *In Concert - Playing the Songs of Elton John and Bernie Taupin. (BBC)*

Below: Performing 'Your Song' on *Top Of The Pops* in 1971 - an odd shot of Elton through a heavily-taped drum kit, and a more traditional view (*BBC*).

Left: Cover for the *17-11-70* live album, 1971. *(David Larkham-Rocket)* *(Sony)*

Right: *Madman Across the Water* cover art, textured to resemble denim, 1971. *(David Larkham - Rocket)*

Left: The *Honky Chateau* album cover with photo by Ed Caraeff, 1972. *(Rocket)*

Above: Interviewed by Bob Harris on the *Old Grey Whistle Test* in early 1973, talking about the setting up of Rocket Records. *(BBC)*

Below: Interviewed on BBCTV *Nationwide* regarding a charity gig to support the National Youth Theatre in 1972 (*BBC*).

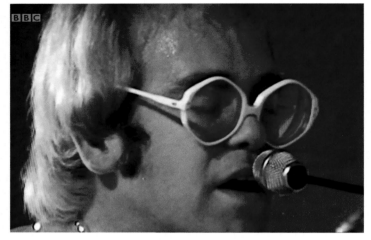

Left: Playing 'Crocodile Rock' at the *Royal Variety Performance* at the London Palladium in 1972 (*BBC*).

Right: Elton moves up a spectacle size in the movie *Tommy*, 1975.

Left: Elton John plays in the back while The Who work in front – *Tommy*, 1975.

Right: Ed Caraeff's striking photo on the *Don't Shoot Me I'm Only the Piano Player* cover. *(Rocket)*

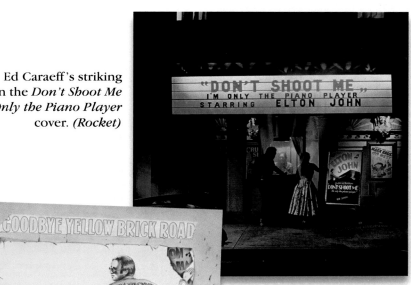

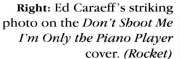

David Larkham's *Goodbye Yellow Brick Road* cover, inspired by a David Bowie *Creem* Magazine cover. *(Rocket)*

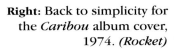

Right: Back to simplicity for the *Caribou* album cover, 1974. *(Rocket)*

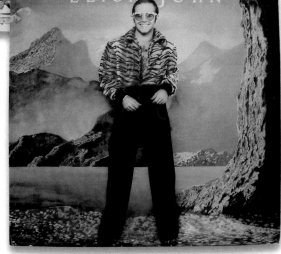

Left: Alan Aldridge's detailed cover illustration for *Captain Fantastic*, drawing on the paintings of Hieronymus Bosch, 1975. *(Rocket)*

Right: Elton John sans surrealistic art for the cover of *Rock Of The Westies*, 1975. *(Rocket)*

Left: The cover for *Here And There* aka *London and New York*, 1976. *(Rocket)*

Above: Another often-seen clip - the promo film for 'Don't Go Breaking My Heart' - recorded for BBCTVs *Top Of The Pops* with Kiki Dee, 1976.(*BBC*)

Below: Promoting the *Captain Fantastic* album on *Countdown* for the ABC, Australia 1975. (*ABC*)

Above & Below: Interviewed by Michael Parkinson for the *Parkinson* Show on the BBC in 1976. Elton talked about playing the piano in a pub, leading to a rather uncomfortable sing-along to 'Maybe It's Because I'm A Londoner' with Parkinson (who is a Yorkshireman) and fellow guest, Michael Caine. (*BBC*)

Left & Below: Elton appeared on the *Morecambe and Wise Christmas Show* on BBC TV in 1977. This much-loved fixture of 1970s Christmas Day entertainment received huge viewing figures, with upwards of 20 million people tuning in. The joke, here, was that Elton turns up for the show, but can never find his way to the right place at the right time, so ends up performing 'Shine On Through' to the cleaning ladies (Eric and Ernie in drag). At the end of the performance, Elton reports that it's that song he would have played on the show, to which Eric retorts 'It's a good job you didn't'. (*BBC*)

Right: Back on *Parkinson* again, in 1977.(*BBC*)

THE ROCKET RECORD COMPANY™

RETURN TO PARADISE
(Elton John/Gary Osborne)(4:12)(Castle)

A

6079 660
SIDE ONE A
STEREO

ELTON JOHN

Produced by Elton John and Clive Franks
for Frank N. Stein Productions Ltd.
From the Rocket LP "A SINGLE MAN"

℗ 1978 William A. Bong Ltd.

ALL RIGHTS OF THE PRODUCER AND OF THE OWNER OF THE WORK REPRODUCED RESERVED. UNAUTHORISED COPYING, HIRING, LENDING, PUBLIC PERFORMANCE AND BROADCASTING OF THIS RECORD PROHIBITED.

Left: The 7" single label for 'Return to Paradise' issued as an A-side in New Zealand, 1978. (*Rocket*)

Right: Label from the 2003, 12" reissue of 'Are You Ready For Love' on London's Southern Fried Records. (*Southern Fried*)

Left: The 7" sleeve for 'Mama Can't Buy You Love' as issued in Spain, 1979.

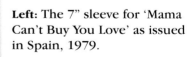

Right: *Blue Moves* cover featuring the painting *The Guardian Readers* by British artist, Patrick Procktor, 1976. *(Rocket)*

Left: The cover for *A Single Man*, with photo taken by Terry O'Neill at Windsor Great Park, Berkshire, England, 1978. *(Rocket)*

Right: *Victim Of Love* album cover with photo by David Bailey, 1979. *(UMC - Mercury)*

Left: Bernie and Maxine's wedding, 1971. (*Daily Mirror*)

Below: Elton and Bernie, September 1970. (*Barrie Wentzell*)

Below: The new band, 1975. Clockwise from top – Ray Cooper, Caleb Quaye, Davey Johnstone, Elton, James Newton-Howard, Kenny Passarelli and Roger Pope.

Sun Go Down on Me'. Add to this, the Christmas single 'Step Into Christmas' which was quickly recorded and released in November 1973, adding to the virtual glut of Elton John product on the market.

Contemporary Tracks:
'Jack Rabbit' (Elton John, Bernie Taupin)
Released as a single B-side, 29 June 1973 (UK), 16 July 1973 (US) b/w 'Saturday Night's Alright for Fighting'.

The 'Saturday Night' B-side had two songs thanks to the brevity of the almost comedic 'Jack Rabbit'. Clocking in at 1m:50s, this swamp country miniature made its point and was gone. Punctuated by the humour of Davey Johnstone's chicken-pickin' licks, we get the cold hard truth of the jackrabbit running through the woods, getting shot and lying in the cold daylight. No more, no less. Elton wrote songs fast anyway, but this couldn't have taken more than a minute.

'Whenever You're Ready (We'll Go Steady Again)' (Elton John, Bernie Taupin)
Released as a single B-side, 29 June 1973 (UK), 16 July 1973 (US) b/w 'Saturday Night's Alright for Fighting'.

Like the jackrabbit, this guy has been left in the cold daylight too. But he doesn't seem to mind. The phrase 'Whenever you're ready, we'll go steady again' sounds more like certainty than forgiveness, which makes the title a bit of a twist. Put to a shuffle rock rhythm, the overall vibe is pretty happy. At only a minute longer than 'Jack Rabbit' - the superior of the two, the writing of this one probably stretched to two minutes. Not that track length and writing duration are mutually conclusive.

'Screw You/Young Man's Blues' (Elton John, Bernie Taupin)
Released as a single B-side, 7 September 1973 (UK), 15 October 1973 (US), b/w 'Goodbye Yellow Brick Road'.

Compared to the previous two songs, there was a lot more meat on the bones of this B-side. Swapping from the verse half-time to the chorus double-time alone gave the track an extra dimension, not to forget the introduction vibe recalling Ringo Starr's 'It Don't Come Easy'. Clearly, the band put time into crafting the backing vocals which suggests the song was a serious contender. But the hopeless lyrical complaints against almost anyone the narrator ever knew were likely what let it down, not to mention the connotation of the original UK title 'Screw You'. The alternative title 'Young Man's Blues' was used on labels and artwork in the USA, but the audio remained the same.

Leroy Gomez performed the saxophone solo and his part on 'Social Disease' later on the same night 'Goodbye Yellow Brick Road' was recorded.

'Step into Christmas' (Elton John, Bernie Taupin)

Released as a single A-side, 26 November 1973 (UK and US), b/w 'Ho! Ho! Ho! Who'd Be a Turkey at Christmas'. UK: 24. AUS: 44. NZ: 38.

Cut along with its B-side at Morgan Studios, London, in November 1973 and released two weeks later, 'Step into Christmas' followed the lead of Wizzard singles like 'See My Baby Jive' and 'Angel Fingers' by following the prevalent Phil Spector-esque wall-of-sound trend.

Though obviously recorded quickly for the Christmas market, the song was musically more worthy than many as a Christmas hit. Hitting a couple of darker chords in spots gave it a little more substance than other competitors that season, like Wizzard's 'I Wish It Could Be Christmas Everyday' or the actual UK Christmas 1973 number one, Slade's 'Merry Xmas Everybody'. Climbing only to 24 in the UK, 'Step into Christmas' did hit number one on the *Billboard* Christmas chart in the USA.

'Ho! Ho! Ho! Who'd Be a Turkey at Christmas' (Elton John, Bernie Taupin)

Released as a single B-side, 26 November 1973 (UK and US), b/w 'Step into Christmas'.

This Christmas knees-up performed its task perfectly. That is, it filled up the plastic on the back of 'Step into Christmas'. But to be fair, the work was always of a high standard, and you'd go a long way to find sloppy playing on any of these records. The piano-playing here is full of Elton's idiosyncratic funky approach, and the rhythm section is pretty tasty too. That feel at that slow speed is harder than it sounds, but Dee Murray and Nigel Olsson could do that stuff in their sleep.

Caribou (1974)

Personnel:

Elton John: vocals, pianos, organ

Billy Hinsche, Bruce Johnston, Davey Johnstone, Clydie King, Sherlie Matthews, Dee Murray, Nigel Olsson, Jessie Mae Smith, Dusty Springfield, Toni Tennille, Carl Wilson: backing vocals

Dee Murray: bass

Nigel Olsson: drums

Davey Johnstone: guitars, mandolin

Chester D. Thompson: Hammond organ

Tower of Power: horn section

Stephen Kupka: baritone saxophone

Lenny Pickett: saxophone, clarinet

Emilio Castillo: tenor saxophone

Mic Gillette: trombone

Greg Adams, Mic Gillette: trumpet

Ray Cooper: percussion

David Hentschel: synthesizer, Mellotron

Recorded: Jan. 1974 at Caribou Ranch, Colorado, Brother Studio, California

Producer: Gus Dudgeon

Engineers: Clive Franks, David Hentschel

Arrangers: Del Newman, Daryl Dragon

Release date: 28 June 1974 (UK), 24 June 1974 (US)

Chart placings: UK: 1, US: 1, CAN: 1, AUS: 1

Passing through Colorado on his massive 1973 tour of the USA, Elton paid a visit to Caribou Ranch at Nederland, home of Jim Guercio's recently constructed recording facility hidden away in the Rocky Mountains. Taking a shine to the place, Elton, Bernie, Gus Dudgeon and band retired to the winter snows of the ranch in January 1974 to commence work on the follow-up to the successful double album.

From some quarters, there was the unrealistic expectation to follow *Goodbye Yellow Brick Road* with something akin to the greatest album of all time. Instead, the resulting *Caribou* was baulked at by many, Gus Dudgeon himself later saying it wasn't all it could have been. The rustic rural surroundings were conducive to work, but the pressure was on, and repeated technical difficulties made the recording process frustrating. The simultaneous writing and recording was a mammoth effort packed into a small time frame of ten days before a scheduled Japanese tour beginning on 1 February at Tokyo's Budokan Theatre.

Elton would later refer to the period as a turning point. Bernie has since alluded to memories of the sessions being fuzzy around the edges - one example being a day when a visiting Stevie Wonder drove him from his ranch cabin to the studio, Bernie realising later that he'd been driven there by a blind man.

A fairly star-studded line-up of accompanying musicians was later to overdub fairy dust onto the tracks, including singers Dusty Springfield and both Carl Wilson and Bruce Johnston of the Beach Boys. Also taking part were the Captain and Tennille (The Captain Daryl Dragon as vocal arranger and Toni Tennille as a background vocalist), and the Tower Of Power horn section, whose contribution added a real finesse to the production.

At one stage the album was to be called *Ol' Pink Eyes Is Back*, in tribute to Frank Sinatra's recently released album *Ol' Blue Eyes Is Back*, but, in the end, titling it after the recording location was deemed appropriate. Any title probably would have done, as subsequent to its release, *Caribou* followed Elton's now well-established pattern of success by becoming, in '70s parlance, a smash. It also spawned two hit singles in 'Don't Let the Sun Go Down on Me' and 'The Bitch Is Back'.

Nominated for Album of the Year at the 1975 Grammy Awards on 1 March, *Caribou*, unfortunately, lost out to Stevie Wonder's *Fulfillingness' First Finale*.

'The Bitch Is Back' (Elton John, Bernie Taupin)

Released as a single A-side, 30 August 1974 (UK), 3 September 1974 (US), b/w 'Cold Highway'. UK: 15. US: 4. CAN: 1. AUS: 53. NZ: 9.

Famously bleeped on many American radio stations, blanket mainstream coverage of the second *Caribou* single was unstoppable. Elton has called it his theme song, christened as such by Bernie's wife Maxine and her exclamation of 'The bitch is back' when Elton arrived one day in one of his bad moods. Basically, it was an in-joke that Bernie fleshed-out into a lyric and an act of pure self-deprecation on Elton's part to gracefully get the joke.

As could be predicted for a song that was often censored whenever its very title sounded, 'The Bitch is Back' attracted only one '70s cover version, on Tina Turner's 1978 album *Rough*. That recording was not a single, but it might as well have been. You'd think by 1978, post the punk explosion, that the censors would have had more relevant meat to salivate over than a fairly mild self-directed pejorative uttered by a pop queen of yesteryear having (at least as we thought then) one last jab at pop's kisser.

Tina's version could have crept through, though clearly the lyrics had been an issue as multiple lines other than the title were considerably changed, virtually to the extent of a partial re-write. Some changes appeared as blatant corrections to lines apparently offensive to someone or other, while other changes seemed to be simple mistakes or mis-hearings. Bernie Taupin has really been given the short end of the stick in this regard, at least in the '70s. Thankfully these sins of lyrical translation were rectified on Turner's re-recording of the song for 1991's *Two Rooms: Celebrating the Songs of Elton John & Bernie Taupin*. Although the change from 'I get high in the evening sniffing pots of glue' to 'I get high just thinkin' 'bout the things I do', remained.

'Pinky' (Elton John, Bernie Taupin)

It's surprising that this accessible gem was never made a hit in a cover version. Largely overlooked and lacking in attention, the song was clearly taken seriously during production considering the prime position it was given in the album sequence. As the lyric says, 'Pinky's as perfect as the fourth of July, Quilted and timeless, Seldom denied'. Its positive attitude sat comfortably in the popular soft rock idiom of the day, but as we've established, there was a lot of Elton product to go around then, and radio station program directors were spoilt for choice with the number of singles being issued alone. Nevertheless, 'Pinky' acted as a kind of third *Caribou* single, receiving just as much general airplay as the album's two singles, at least here in New Zealand.

'Grimsby' (Elton John, Bernie Taupin)

In contrast to *Goodbye Yellow Brick Road*, one thing *Caribou* can be praised for is the sense of humour that occasionally bangs on the surface underside. Another potential single, though possibly relevant only to the British, the sharp and pointy 'Grimsby' had ironic ambitions of Beach Boys greatness in its glorification of the Lincolnshire seaside port. Such musical praise would have caused little harm to the industry-focused locale, but unfortunately, the ongoing Cod Wars *did*. By 1976, the port of Grimsby was enduring an industrial regression which irreparably affected employment, ultimately smudging the song's shine and denting its brittle exterior.

'Dixie Lily' (Elton John, Bernie Taupin)

Elton wasn't overly happy with some of his *Caribou* vocals, and 'Dixie Lily' was the one vocal he did redo after leaving the ranch. The southern-showboat dedication was another album deep-cut destined for the greatness of mainstream radio exposure, at least in Australasia where it was given multiple daily spins.

American country singer Roy Drusky had a top 50 hit with it in 1974, the same year British skiffler Lonnie Donegan included a frantic bluegrass version on the *Lonnie Donegan Meets Leinemann* album. Both versions demonstrated questionable vocals but superlative musicianship. In Donegan's case, the band was moving so fast he could barely fit the words in. But thankfully, all lyrics were intact across the board. Hurrah!

'Solar Prestige A Gammon' (Elton John, Bernie Taupin)

With a history of many false lyric interpretations tickling Elton and Bernie pink, Bernie threw 'Solar Prestige A Gammon' into the mix to flummox those insistent on uncovering hidden meanings. The language was nonsense, but he added several fish names as red herrings! In fact, herring was one of the names.

As if not to be beaten, one uncoverer of hidden meanings came up with the idea that the song title was an anagram of 'Elton's Program Is A Game'. There were apparently no distances the scholarly students of Taupin's muse wouldn't travel to shine a light on something that wasn't there.

In reality it was Elton's complimentary chords, illuminated by a continental-sounding accordion, that shone light upon the lyric, providing unlikely emotion and even causing listener sympathy to whatever might be the issue at play in the non-story - which just goes to show that the appropriate musical approach will put a spin on any lyric, nonsense or not. If anything, the fish references tied the bouncy and ambitious sea shanty in with 'Grimsby' being the first, and 'Dixie Lily' the second of a trifecta of water songs that were the nucleus of side one.

'You're So Static' (Elton John, Bernie Taupin)
Coming across like an edgy cinematic leftover from *Goodbye Yellow Brick Road*, this blunt warning of a seemingly unavoidable New York hustle is the second of the two pieces of grit that bookend side one. It places you firmly back on shore as surely as 'The Bitch is Back' led you from it.

But there's more to it. In many ways 'You're So Static' is the instrumental pinnacle of *Caribou*. Harmonically exotic, the piano part lap-dances enticingly around the chords, punctuated by the soulful stabs and piercing arpeggios of the Tower of Power horn section. Davey Johnstone's guitar lines, fed through a spinning Leslie cabinet, create a sense of disorientation throughout. It all builds to a dizzying frenzy that doesn't let up, leaving the narrator spent, and the listener washed-up and well-situated for the further landlocked adventures waiting on side two.

'I've Seen the Saucers' (Elton John, Bernie Taupin)
'I've Seen the Saucers' was one of the last tracks to convey a specific dark mood that made itself known on *Madman Across the Water*, parts of *Don't Shoot Me I'm Only the Piano Player*, and all but permeated *Goodbye Yellow Brick Road*. That mood was never re-captured in quite the same way again, except perhaps for the coming 'Someone Saved My Life Tonight' which pretty much closed the door on that haunted bleeding indigo flavour forever. After 1975, Elton's music, and indeed the musical remainder of the '70s, changed entirely, for better or worse depending on your viewpoint.

But back in 1974, the literature of ufology was all the rage amongst a certain crowd who pored over books like J. Allen Hynek's *The UFO Experience*, Erich Von Daniken's *Chariots of the Gods?* and Bruce Cathie's *Harmonic 695*. This was all before the UFO craze lost its mojo by finding the mainstream and becoming ultra-commercialised through movies like *Star Wars* and *Close Encounters of the Third Kind*.

So 'I've Seen the Saucers' could stand for its time as a singularly serious and sincere homage to the subject - a homage that was minus any irony or aspects of novelty that would infiltrate many pop songs that landed after the mainstream sci-fi bubble finally burst in 1977. Perhaps the song shares this honour with Klaatu's 'Calling Occupants of Interplanetary Craft', another sincere offering in its original incarnation, however partially pillaged it may have been by the beautifully produced but somewhat mocking Carpenters hit version of 1977.

Objectively speaking, 'I've Seen the Saucers' can simply be described as plainly beautiful and criminally overlooked. Maybe it was underplayed. Maybe after 'Space Oddity', 'Life on Mars?' and 'Rocket Man', the space thing felt like it was done. It's probably just fate that some songs, being borne at the hands of the prolific, will starve for attention, lost amongst the endless competition of their greater and lesser siblings.

'Stinker' (Elton John, Bernie Taupin)

In its down-and-dirty slow blues shuffle, the neglected 'Stinker' carried harmonic shades of the 1973 Beach Boys hit 'Sail On, Sailor'. The two songs shared verse melody similarities, but 'Stinker' was meaner and grittier. It also acted as a kind of stylistic pre-cursor to the fabulous 'Heart in the Right Place' from Elton's 1981 album *The Fox*, and even 'The Wasteland' from 2001's *Songs From the West Coast*.

The track cooked as it progressed, getting increasingly cloudy once two guitars, organ and horns were added with the rhythm section, all wailing simultaneously in the final choruses. But the track was masterfully mixed and deserved album inclusion from the playing alone, featuring as it did the mighty Tower of Power horn section and additionally their organist, Chester Thompson.

'Stinker', despite the central character's poor self-image, acted as a kind of mood-settler, bringing the listener down to earth after the suspension of disbelief wrought by 'I've Seen the Saucers'. Sure, the pot might have contained better songs, but this was a musician's jam – dignified and unpretentious.

'Don't Let the Sun Go Down on Me' (Elton John, Bernie Taupin)

Released as a single A-side, 20 May 1974 (UK and US), b/w 'Sick City'. UK: 16. US: 2. CAN: 1. AUS: 13. NZ: 5.

Elton had recorded many ballads, but 'Don't Let the Sun Go Down on Me' was the first that sounded like art was being edged out, and commerce was taking over. 'Candle in the Wind' kept its cool with the dark overtones characteristic of the album that housed it, and 'Goodbye Yellow Brick Road' was seductive with its winding chord passages and abstract statements. But this first *Caribou* single had a different attitude altogether.

There used to be ballads, but now what came to be known as big ballads were appearing. A forerunner was Paul McCartney and Wings' 1973 hit 'My Love', and Barbra Streisand's hit that year, 'The Way We Were', which straddled a line between traditional easy-listening and big ballad. Surprisingly, UK glam rockers Slade struck big ballad gold in 1974 with 'Everyday', which really came out of left field. The slow track couldn't contain their usual exuberance, which still came barrelling to the surface, turning the ballad to big. You could even trace this line back to David Bowie's 1971 *Hunky Dory* masterpiece 'Life on Mars?'. Who's to say a ballad has to be a love song? Although, one of that song's major influences, the Frank Sinatra standard 'My Way', could be considered to be the ultimate big ballad.

The big ballad was a development, a new strain in the pop DNA. Even Stevie Wonder hadn't yet risked a ballad as a single since re-signing with Motown in 1971, so 'Don't Let the Sun Go Down on Me' stood as a big, fresh, shiny lump of lovey-dovey goo, ripe for radio ears to take in. And take it they did, to number one in Canada and even to the 1975 Grammy Awards where it was nominated for both Record of the Year and Best Pop Vocal Performance.

Elton was unsure about his vocal at first, doubting it was worthy of album inclusion. But the final record spoke for itself, and quite loudly thanks to both Del Newman's dynamic arrangement for the Tower of Power horns, and the backing vocal group including Toni Tennille and the Beach Boys' Carl Wilson and Bruce Johnston - arranged by Johnston and the Captain, Daryl Dragon.

The inherent musical influence that comes from recording on a different continent might have played a part in birthing the new sound too. Also, with the band being under pressure to record fast due to an upcoming tour, and doubts about some of the material, whatever could be done to give the tracks extra power and energy was well worth the effort. In this case, it paid off for the initial single and in a second run as a mega chart hit in the George Michael-led duet from 1991.

'Ticking' (Elton John, Bernie Taupin)
Unfortunately, this shocking story of mass murder and police vengeance is more relevant now than it was at the time of its composition. It has been suggested that the story was based on the perpetrator of the 1966 University of Texas clock tower killings, but generally, it could be applied to any metaphorical ticking time bomb.

This solo masterpiece holds the dual honour of harbouring *Caribou*'s darkest corner and displaying Elton's finest performance on the album. Where the cinematic *Goodbye Yellow Brick Road* stopped short of a sonic newsreel, *Caribou* provided one in this fearless social commentary. But Bernie and Elton were at the point where they could do no wrong and could write and sing about whatever they pleased. There were critics, sure, it went with the territory, but for now, the Captain and the kid were riding the tiger, fast approaching the top of the hill.

Contemporary Tracks:
'Sick City' (Elton John, Bernie Taupin)
Released as a single B-side, 20 May 1974 (UK and US), b/w 'Don't Let the Sun Go Down on Me'.
Released as a single A-side, 1974 (FRA), b/w 'Cold Highway'.
This snazzy funk B-side recorded at Caribou Ranch was left off *Caribou*, perhaps due to its frank and suggestive lyrics detailing the showbiz lifestyle of

groupie accoutrements. The cut was, nevertheless, issued as a single in France. The one-time rarity is a finely cut gem that shines due to the gorgeous Tower of Power horn arrangement and what I'd describe as bassist Dee Murray's finest performance on an Elton record to that date.

'Cold Highway' (Elton John, Bernie Taupin)

Released as a single B-side, 30 August 1974 (UK), 3 September 1974 (US), b/w 'The Bitch Is Back'.

This and the above B-side were a real one-two punch, with this one being the knockout. Both lyrics tackled difficult subjects and were supported by superlative chord changes. Clearly, Elton was on a roll that could have been more productive, but the album recording deadline was approaching, and a tour of Japan was looming.

With the furore that became the 'The Bitch Is Back' radio censorship debacle, its stylish B-side was considered as an alternative for airplay by some stations. The chorus certainly had a hook, but the verse lyrics were dark. The character speaking is addressing a dead friend, possibly a celebrity. The song could easily apply to Jim Morrison or Jimi Hendrix, but my guess is that it was a dedication to someone Bernie knew, at least as an acquaintance, in the '60s.

'Pinball Wizard' (Pete Townshend)

Released as a single A-side, 12 March 1976 (UK), February 1976 (AUS and NZ), b/w 'Harmony'. UK: 7. AUS: 88.

In April 1974, this glamorous and energetic version of the Pete Townshend classic was recorded for the *Tommy* movie in which Elton had a role as the Pinball Wizard. His core band were retained for the session which was produced by Gus Dudgeon at The Who's Ramport Studios in London.

A top ten in the UK, the track was issued only as a promotional single in the USA and barely scraped the chart in Australia. It nevertheless gained a fair amount of popularity through generous airplay in New Zealand, becoming a turntable hit there.

The *Tommy* role of Pinball Wizard was originally offered to Rod Stewart. Consulting Elton on the offer, he was sincerely advised against doing it. Then after some begging from Pete Townshend, Elton ended up taking the role himself. He felt it was the thing to do, Townshend having been an early supporter, often appearing in the audience at Elton's early shows.

The entire experience was a positive one, Elton describing working on director Ken Russell's surreal project as like being on *Top of the Pops* with huge shoes.

Captain Fantastic and the Brown Dirt Cowboy (1975)

Personnel:
Elton John: vocals, pianos, clavinet, harpsichord, Mellotron, synthesizer
Davey Johnstone, Dee Murray, Nigel Olsson: backing vocals
Dee Murray: bass
Nigel Olsson: drums
Davey Johnstone: guitars, mandolin, electric piano
Ray Cooper: percussion
David Hentschel: synthesizer
Recorded: June/July 1974 at Caribou Ranch, Colorado
Producer: Gus Dudgeon
Engineers: Jeff Guercio, Mark Guercio
Arranger: Gene Page
Release date: 23 May 1975 (UK), 19 May 1975 (US)
Chart placings: UK: 2, US: 1, CAN: 1, AUS: 1

In July 1974, Elton, Nigel Olsson and Davey Johnstone were aboard the cruise liner *S.S. France* travelling from Southampton to New York. Elton was attempting to write the songs for *Captain Fantastic and the Brown Dirt Cowboy* which was to be recorded in the coming weeks back at the Caribou Ranch. Opportunities to use the ship's music room were at a premium due to a rehearsing opera singer, who was keeping the primary amenity, the grand piano, constantly occupied. So, the songs were written when the piano was free, usually during the lunch hour.

Soon after the album's release, Elton was to tell an Australian interviewer in jest that the album was a story about how he and Bernie got together, so he wouldn't have to answer the question again – he could just give you the album instead. In all seriousness, it was indeed an autobiography covering the time period from Elton and Bernie's meeting, up to the point of making the *Empty Sky* album. The narrative covered many events including experiences with music publishers, disappointments over song refusals, relationships and even songwriting itself.

The songs were written in the album order from start to finish, which was a new way of working. Elton said it was painless work since he was able to relate to every lyric so easily. The songs also dealt with the two writers and their separate experiences – Bernie and his homesickness for Lincolnshire, and Elton going through a relationship that spawned the album's only single, 'Someone Saved My Life Tonight'. Bernie would usually write very quickly, but he'd spent more time on these, working on multiple lyrics at once, going back and forth between them. It was all a new exercise that paid off.

Caribou was paying off too. Its platinum-level sales were reported to Elton while he was onboard the ship (though platinum certification was not officially introduced until 1976). By the time recording began at the ranch, spirits were high. This project was more pleasurable to work on than the last, the band now being accustomed to the studio and its idiosyncrasies. On the sessions, this time, were house engineers Jeff and Mark Guercio. Musicians were kept to a minimum, with all parts being played by the core band along with David Hentschel on synthesizer.

By this point, Elton's music dominated the commercial airwaves. Skimming across the radio dial in America there would barely be two minutes without an Elton track being played somewhere. One Los Angeles station dubbed itself 'Your Number One Elton John station'. Another claimed, 'We play more Elton John than anybody', and a New York station decided it was 'Your official Elton John spot on the dial'.

So it was no surprise when *Captain Fantastic and the Brown Dirt Cowboy* was declared a gold record before its 19 May 1975 release date. But it was a surprise when it was officially declared the first album ever to come straight in at number one in the USA - although this had occurred in 1948 when the album chart only had five discs in it, so that didn't really count. Eventually, when Elton was presented on camera with the platinum record for sales of 1.4 million copies, he exclaimed at being at a loss for where to put them all.

'Captain Fantastic and the Brown Dirt Cowboy' (Elton John, Bernie Taupin)

The subtle country-tinged opening of the title track barely suggested what it would become by the chorus. On one side it presented a kind of 'Texan Love Song'-era Elton, which moved suddenly to a more rock attitude anticipating *Rock of the Westies* songs like 'Yell Help' and 'Street Kids'.

The lyric clearly outlined the two main characters, but the album was never intended to be commercial or even necessarily yield a hit single, so some passages conveyed their message through a mixture of abstraction and metaphor. Many references would have a more obvious meaning to the writers than the listener. Nevertheless, a line like 'For we were spinning out our lines, Walking on the wire', spoke for itself as a clear reference to entering the songwriting business.

At times Elton has spoken of the album as their best work and has claimed to get emotional singing the title track.

'Tower of Babel' (Elton John, Bernie Taupin)

Considering the songs were written and recorded in sequence, it's interesting that you still naturally get what would be a phenomenon in the construction of any album; that is, one of the strongest tracks near the beginning.

This track is noteworthy for the instrumental mid-section alone, with its dominating bass line that sucks in all the other instrumentation. Elton's voice is in fine form, 'Tower of Babel' perhaps being the defining vocal of his entire career.

In 1975, a *Creem* magazine writer theorised that 'Tower of Babel' was about the 1974 death of Average White Band drummer Robbie McIntosh, an event

Bernie allegedly witnessed. An advance glance at the promo material might have set the writer straight, but he did well to glean something so specific from a lyric so abstract, however off-topic his theory might have been. The majority of the album's lyrics were abstract and 'Tower of Babel' was one of its most inscrutable. But the enticing lyric and its suggestive adventures of carnivorous and untroubled risk-takers suggested an intellectual penetration of the naivety Bernie claimed to personify at the inception of the partnership. 'Tower of Babel' was a song he and Elton could never have written pre-1970 despite having lived through the lyric. Likewise, could the song have been written if they hadn't experienced their subsequent success? By 1975 they'd done and seen it all and 'Tower of Babel' carried the weight of the early '70s as surely as it did the buoyancy of the late '60s.

'Bitter Fingers' (Elton John, Bernie Taupin)
Contracted in the early days to churn out pretty commercial tunes for potential dispersal to various recording artists, Elton, and particularly Bernie, tired quickly of the scenario. This is reflected as frustration in the up-tempo and sprightly 'Bitter Fingers'. The chorus lines, 'It seems to me a change is really needed, I'm sick of tra-la-las and la-de-das', make it painfully clear.

But the verses show evidence of another four anonymous narrators, their requests typical of those made regularly to the pair on London's Tin Pan Alley, Denmark Street. One request line was, 'We need a tune to open our season at Southend'. But verse two began with a couplet that appeared to reflect Elton, stating, 'I like the warm blue flame, The hazy heat it brings, It loosens up the muscles and forces you to sing'.

Techniques were mixed in this concoction. The two verses differed in their musical structure, which suggests Elton wrote the music to the lyrics as they were written as opposed to moving lines around to fit his melody.

It's a song that could have made a great single were it not for the general obscurity of the subject matter. But it didn't seem to matter when 'Bitter Fingers' received the most rapturous applause at the album's advance playback press shindig at Media Sound Studios in New York.

'Tell Me When the Whistle Blows' (Elton John, Bernie Taupin)
Having written string arrangements for soul artists such as Barry White and the Love Unlimited Orchestra, the Los Angeles-born Gene Page now put his hand to two songs from the *Captain Fantastic* sessions - 'Philadelphia Freedom' and 'Tell Me When the Whistle Blows'. The former was to be an additional single separate to the album, in the Philadelphia soul style. The latter song shared the soul bent, which made it sit a little stylistically out of character with the rest of the album material. But Bernie's lyrical memory here of homesickness and his early days on the road in England was appropriate to the style, thanks to lines like, 'Has this country kid still got his soul?'

'Someone Saved My Life Tonight' (Elton John, Bernie Taupin)

Released as a single A-side, May 1975 (UK), 23 June 1975 (US), b/w 'House of Cards'. UK: 22. US: 1. CAN: 2. AUS: 54. NZ: 13.

By this stage in the game, Bernie Taupin rarely heard newly-written songs before the recordings were finished, and that was the case with those from *Captain Fantastic*. So when Gus Dudgeon played him some of the finished tracks, Bernie came at them to a large extent equivalent to any new listener, and to another extent, captivated in one way or another due to his personal involvement in the compositions. He loved the songs, but when 'Someone Saved My Life Tonight' played, he was overcome and had to leave the room. He has claimed he found the track to be so extraordinary, that he couldn't take it.

As mentioned in the entry for 'I've Seen the Saucers', 'Someone Saved My Life Tonight', although we didn't know it, represented the closing of a chapter in Elton's sound. It was the last lap of a particular dark spirit that characterised many of his early ballads. A line could be traced through 'Rocket Man', 'Have Mercy on the Criminal', many *Goodbye Yellow Brick Road* tracks (but specifically 'I've Seen That Movie Too'), 'I've Seen the Saucers', and now what would become the sole *Captain Fantastic* single. Play those songs in sequence, and it's plain to hear. It's not because they're all slow, it's something more intangible. A similar spirit was present on Kiki Dee's haunting 1973 single 'Amoureuse', which featured Dee Murray and Davey Johnstone, so I thought it might be down to his guitar volume technique during performance, but that sound was absent from 'Someone Saved My Life Tonight', so we can fall back on the intangible. It's better not to know anyway. Some things don't need a name.

Whatever it was, it bled out on this song that purged the past more than any other on the album. In this case, a past that contained Linda Woodrow, a woman Elton met on a rainy Sheffield Christmas when performing with Long John Baldry. Before long she moved to London, and they shared a flat with Bernie in a dismal part of the East End. For six stormy months, no songs were written, while Elton and Linda planned to marry. It all culminated in the well-known cry for help with the oven gas on low and the windows open. One night at the London club, the Bag of Nails, three weeks before the scheduled big day, John Baldry talked Elton out of marrying her. After what Elton described as 'Two days of hell' passed, the song's famous truck, that in fact was a Ford Cortina containing his step-dad Fred, arrived to take him home.

The lengthy single, which Elton refused to allow to be edited, officially hit number four in *Billboard*, but number one in *Cashbox* in the now familiar pattern. The poignant re-telling took Elton's work to the ears of millions once again, along with that stunning drum sound and what Davey Johnstone later described as the band's finest backing vocal work of all.

'(Gotta Get A) Meal Ticket' (Elton John, Bernie Taupin)

Side two's opener was written on Monday 22 July 1974 aboard the *SS France*. Elton managed to wangle the music room piano which was constantly occupied by the rehearsing opera singer. In this case, she removed herself and commenced battle from a piano the floor above. Half an hour later, Elton had the song that would eventually stand in for a non-existent second single.

The bitter song, which was the heaviest number on *Captain Fantastic*, was about the jealousy of seeing others become successful while you're still struggling yourself. The recorded track, Elton's favourite from the album at the time, anticipated the rock style that would become the cornerstone of 1975's *Rock of the Westies*.

'Better Off Dead' (Elton John, Bernie Taupin)

'Better Off Dead' was another song Bernie didn't hear for the first time until after it was recorded. He wrote the lyric about his and Elton's experiences hitting the streets of London's West End after late-night recording sessions for *Empty Sky*. Imagining the song in the style of American folk singer-songwriter John Prine, Bernie left a note to that effect on the bottom of the lyric when he gave it to Elton. But what came out was something very different, more along the lines of a Gilbert and Sullivan comic opera.

Eclecticism had long been an element of the band's work, but 'Better Off Dead' came from left field more than any of the other new tracks. The song's mere 2m:38s demonstrated many strengths, including the deep richness of Nigel Olsson's Slingerland drum kit, here subjected to a slap-back echo recalling some of Phil Spector's John Lennon productions. Another highlight was the band's detailed and up-front backing vocal arrangement in the middle section. It was all a long way from Bernie's original idea for a folk song, and it took him a moment to warm to the reality.

'Writing' (Elton John, Bernie Taupin)

Captain Fantastic approaches its end with a triad of songs with lyrics addressing the act of songwriting. In the early days, Bernie lived with Elton and his mother, Sheila, in their upstairs apartment in London's Northwood Hills. The up-tempo and bubbly 'Writing' was written specifically about those times when the two were discovering how each other worked. Bernie would be in the bedroom writing lyrics while Elton was at the living room's white upright piano, writing to the previous lyric he'd been given. This is the piano he's pictured sitting at on the back cover of the 1975 edition of *Empty Sky*.

The recording of this light-hearted but poignant song ended up as somewhat of a showcase for Davey Johnstone. Not only was his tasteful lead guitar harmony work to the fore throughout, but he also played the Fender Rhodes electric piano on the track.

'We All Fall in Love Sometimes' (Elton John, Bernie Taupin)

The first of a closing pair of ballads explores how Elton and Bernie spent a long time attempting to write a song that had some kind of a spark that really moved them. The first verse appears to refer to sitting around with the radio going, frustrated and hearing Elvis Presley's 'Can't Help Falling in Love', which shares the opening phrase, 'Wise men say'. If it doesn't refer to that, it's a believable image.

The longed-for spark suddenly appeared the night Elton unveiled 'Your Song' for the first time. After all the rubbish they felt they'd written together, they finally felt like something had changed and something was going to happen. They'd broken through the glass ceiling. And to quote another cliché, you write a hundred songs, throw them away and then start again – then you're a songwriter. 'Your Song' was the start-again point.

'Curtains' (Elton John, Bernie Taupin)

The previous song referred to 'Your Song', but the final one specifically name-checked 'Scarecrow', the very first John/Taupin composition, written before they'd even met. 'Curtains', the third ballad from the album, brought everything full circle and was the summation of all that came before and the leaping-off point for all that was about to unfold. 'I held a dandelion that said the time had come, To leave upon the wind, Not to return'.

The tastefully placed final phrase was 'Once upon a time' – appropriate as it symbolised the beginning of a new era. This led directly into a long and repetitive vocal hook section that would give the finale of the Beatles' 'Hey Jude' a run for its money.

The tale of *Captain Fantastic and the Brown Dirt Cowboy* ended at the point where the intrepid two were about to embark on their first American trip. The story was picked up on the 2006 album, *The Captain and the Kid*, which was a respectable sequel, and along with 2001's *Songs from the West Coast*, was quite a return to Elton's '70s form.

Contemporary Tracks:
'Dogs in the Kitchen' (Bernie Taupin)

Not a song as such but a poem Bernie wrote which pre-empted the idea to write an album about their lives. The poem was included in the booklet that came in the *Captain Fantastic* album sleeve.

'Lucy in the Sky with Diamonds' (John Lennon, Paul McCartney)

Released as a single A-side, 15 November 1974 (UK), 18 November 1974 (US), b/w 'One Day at a Time'. UK: 10. US: 1. CAN: 1. AUS: 3. NZ: 2.

After watching the *Yellow Submarine* movie on TV one night, Bernie suggested that The Beatles' 'Lucy in the Sky with Diamonds' might be a good song to play in concert. The band performed the song at a Watford Football Club benefit show and at the Royal Festival Hall concert, part of which would eventually make up side one of the *Here and There* live album. The song went down extremely well.

Just before the recording of *Captain Fantastic*, Elton visited John Lennon who was working on his *Walls and Bridges* album in New York, played piano and sang harmony vocals on 'Whatever Gets You Thru the Night' and then made a bet with Lennon that the song would hit number one. Lennon was sceptical, so Elton made him promise that if the song did hit the top spot, Lennon would join him onstage at Madison Square Garden in November. Lennon, who was all but retired from performing live, agreed, not believing the song would be a hit.

After that recording session, Elton told Lennon he'd like to record one of his songs and asked him what one he'd like him to do. Lennon suggested 'Lucy in the Sky' because no one had ever covered it. So, the decision was made to record the song.

Lennon was about to make a trip to Los Angeles, so Elton invited him to stop at Caribou on the way back to record 'Lucy in the Sky' during the *Captain Fantastic* sessions. Lennon agreed. Singing and playing guitar on the choruses, he was credited on the single as Dr Winston O'Boogie & his Reggae Guitars.

Shortly thereafter, Lennon's single of 'Whatever Gets You Thru the Night' indeed hit number one in America. Elton's 'Lucy in the Sky' single also hit the top, making it the most successful Beatles cover recording to that point. Lennon kept his end of the deal and appeared with Elton and band at Madison Square Garden on Thanksgiving night, Thursday 28 November 1974. It would be Lennon's last ever concert appearance. There they performed and recorded the two songs along with the Beatles' number 'I Saw Her Standing There'. All three tracks appeared on a DJM single and a European album release in 1981, eventually being included on the 1995 Mercury and 1996 Rocket reissues of the *Here and There* live album.

In late 1976, Elton's cover of 'Lucy in the Sky' was included in Tony Palmer's *All This and World War II* - a movie that played Beatles cover songs over World War II footage. Soundtrack producer Lou Reizner intended to add an orchestra to the track, so it fit with the mood of much of the album, but Elton refused to let them touch it. As it happened, the movie bombed, but the soundtrack was more successful.

'One Day at a Time' (John Lennon)
Released as a single B-side, 15 November 1974 (UK), 18 November 1974 (US), b/w 'One Day at a Time'.
On his 1973 *Mind Games* album, John Lennon performed this song almost flippantly as if to undermine it. Elton took it a little more seriously, simplifying the chords, so the song shone through more. He enhanced the choruses by singing in three-part harmony with himself, effectively making the song more memorable and its charm more obvious.

'Philadelphia Freedom' (Elton John, Bernie Taupin)
Released as a single A-side, 28 February 1975 (UK), 24 February 1975 (US), b/w 'I Saw Her Standing There'. UK: 12. US: 1. CAN: 1. AUS: 4. NZ: 2.

For 'Philadelphia Freedom', American composer and arranger Gene Page was enlisted to provide a string arrangement that reflected the Philadelphia soul style of hit producers Kenny Gamble and Leon Huff. The song itself was written for tennis player Billie Jean King's team, the Philadelphia Freedoms. The single was a huge success, almost matching that of 'Lucy in the Sky with Diamonds', released a mere three months before.

'I Saw Her Standing There' (Live) (John Lennon, Paul McCartney)

Released as a single B-side, 28 February 1975 (UK), 24 February 1975 (US), b/w 'Philadelphia Freedom'. AUS: 4.

Released as a single A-side, 13 March 1981 (UK), b/w 'Whatever Gets You Thru the Night' (Live) and 'Lucy in the Sky with Diamonds' (Live). UK: 40. AUS: 81.

Recorded live with John Lennon as guest on Thanksgiving night, Thursday 28 November 1974 at Madison Square Garden, New York. In Australia, this B-side was given an equivalent chart entry to the A-side, 'Philadelphia Freedom'. See a more detailed description of this B-side in the section on the *Here and There* live album.

'House of Cards' (Elton John, Bernie Taupin)

Released as a single B-side, May 1975 (UK), 23 June 1975 (US), b/w 'House of Cards'.

The B-side of 'Someone Saved My Life Tonight' kept up the tradition of superlative Elton B-sides. The country-folk song was hook-laden throughout and possibly even worthy A-side material, had it been a bit happier. But compared to powerful and contemporary-sounding yardstick singles like 'Lucy in the Sky with Diamonds' and 'Philadelphia Freedom', it sounded tired. Probably not a fair comparison to make, but it's another fine piece of work that suffered from being surrounded by superior material.

Rock of the Westies (1975)

Personnel:
Elton John: vocals, piano
Kiki Dee, Clive Franks, Davey Johnstone, Kenny Passarelli, Caleb Quaye, Labelle,
Sarah Dash, Nona Hendryx, Patti Labelle: backing vocals
Kenny Passarelli: bass
Roger Pope: drums
Davey Johnstone, Caleb Quaye: guitars, mandolin, banjo
James Newton-Howard: keyboards
Ray Cooper: percussion
Recorded: June/July 1975 at Caribou Ranch, Colorado
Producer: Gus Dudgeon
Engineers: Jeff Guercio, Mark Guercio
Release date: 4 October 1975 (UK), 20 October 1975 (US)
Chart placings: UK: 5, US: 1, CAN: 1, AUS: 4

For a number of weeks, Elton agonised over changing his band. He wanted to
expand the number of musicians and aim for a more rock-orientated sound.
Whether to remove band members that had been with him through all of his
greatest successes was a decision not taken lightly.

The rhythm section was a key area for consideration. Hookfoot drummer
Roger Pope, who'd played on early Elton albums, was brought into the fold.
On Joe Walsh's recommendation, Elton hired bassist Kenny Passarelli, ex of
the Stephen Stills band and Joe Walsh's Barnstorm. Davey Johnstone and Ray
Cooper were retained, which left the matter of expanding guitar and keyboards.

Guitarist Caleb Quaye, who'd been a cornerstone of Elton's early recordings,
was invited on-board, agreeing on the condition that he would never have to
play 'Crocodile Rock'. Elton concurred.

Canadian keyboardist, David Foster, breaking into the upper echelon
having recently contributed to George Harrison's *Extra Texture* album, was
considered as an additional player but was passed over.

Los Angeles-based keyboardist and arranger James Newton-Howard, fresh
from recording sessions for Ringo Starr and Carly Simon, was given the
opportunity to audition thanks to his manager. A wonderfully clandestine
meeting was set up for Newton–Howard who was told to wait outside a
hamburger joint on the corner of L.A.'s Doheny and Sunset at a certain time
and look for a purple Rolls Royce. The vehicle appeared, and James was told
to follow. In his beat-up old station wagon, he followed the Rolls up into the
Hollywood Hills to a mansion, where he was taken into a living room and told
to wait. While waiting, he saw three copies of his own 1974 solo album sitting
on a coffee table. In walked Elton who greeted him and then played him the
entire *Captain Fantastic* album which was about to come out. Not much was
said between the two but when the album was finished Elton said, 'Well you've
got the gig if you want it', and that was it. James had four days to learn 35

songs before flying out for two weeks of rehearsal in Amsterdam.

The new band's debut was to 80,000 people at Wembley Stadium, London, for the Midsummer Music concert on Saturday 21 June 1975. Joining them onstage as a guest was Steely Dan and Doobie Brothers guitarist Jeff 'Skunk' Baxter, but not before an all-day concert of sets from Stackridge, Rufus, Joe Walsh, Eagles and The Beach Boys. Sitting in the royal box were Harry Nilsson, John Entwistle, Ringo Starr, Paul McCartney and fellow Wings members. The band played a set of favourites, including 'I Saw Her Standing There' and 'Lucy in the Sky with Diamonds' in honour of the two ex-Beatles. Elton and band followed that set by performing the complete *Captain Fantastic and the Brown Dirt Cowboy* album which was then enjoying its huge moment in the spotlight. Encores were 'Pinball Wizard' and 'Saturday Night's Alright for Fighting'.

The following day, Elton flew out to the States to prepare for a month at Caribou Ranch recording the new album, which would come to be titled *Rock of the Westies*. The idea was for the musicians to record simultaneously as a unit, with minimal, if any, overdubs from the core band. This was accomplished, but producer Gus Dudgeon was to upset the apple cart by requesting that Kenny Passarelli re-record his bass parts after the fact. The fretless bass sound had been the apparent source of some problem that was evident only to Gus's ears. This caused some consternation. In the end, three of the original bass tracks were kept – 'Medley', 'Street Kids' and 'Feed Me'. On Gus's suggestion, the rest were re-recorded on a Hohner fretted bass that had been a gift to him from Paul McCartney. Passarelli noted the bass's high string action as being particularly troublesome.

But the sessions, in general, were a positive experience for all involved. Band favourites in the course of recording were 'I Feel Like a Bullet (In the Gun of Robert Ford)', 'Medley (Yell Help, Wednesday Night, Ugly)' and 'Billy Bones and the White Bird'. The album was originally to be titled *Bottled and Brained*, after a phrase from the song 'Street Kids', but it was decided to go with a pun on 'west of the Rockies'.

Rock of the Westies was dedicated to Nigel Olsson and Dee Murray, and like *Captain Fantastic*, debuted at number one in the USA, going gold upon its October 1975 release. Issued of course on MCA Records in the USA and Canada, *Rock of the Westies* was the last album of new Elton material released on DJM Records in other territories. The coming live album *Here and There* was to fulfil Elton's contractual obligation to DJM, thereafter freeing him to record for his own label, Rocket Records.

'Medley (Yell Help, Wednesday Night, Ugly)' (Elton John, Bernie Taupin, Davey Johnstone)

In talking to bassist Kenny Passarelli for this book, one question was whether the three seemingly distinct songs that make up this medley were written separately and joined as one later, or were actually written as one at the piano. He confirmed the latter, saying the three lyrics were looked at, Elton instantly deciding to combine them. The fact that 'Wednesday Night' and 'Ugly' share subtle melodic and rhythmic motifs would support this. It had always been obvious to me that the three pieces were at least not recorded separately and edited together.

But surgery was required to an extent. Backing vocals were provided by American R&B vocal group, Labelle. Elton had first come into contact with Patti Labelle when backing her vocal group, the Bluebelles, as a member of Bluesology on a 1966 tour of England. After Patti, Nona Hendryx and Sarah Dash recorded backing vocals on Elton's *Rock of the Westies* medley, part of their performance was accidentally erased from the master tape. This is evident in the section after 'Ugly' up until the stop at 5m:08s. It's in that space that Gus Dudgeon attempted a repair, singing the 'do do do' parts himself. I'd guess the fact he went back and also sang those around Labelle's parts earlier in the track would have been to make his later vocal section seem logical and like it belonged. Smart thinking. I never noticed the girls' parts missing from that section, but since I discovered this fact, I find their absence sticks out like three sore thumbs.

Something was clearly amiss at mixing time too, as the left-hand side of the backing vocals drops out for two seconds at 2m:27s. This would suggest a possible manual mix as opposed to automation, which had become all the rage by then. Things like that could easily happen in a manual mix, but either way, it didn't really matter. The focus was on the composition and the performance, and both were superlative in this instance.

'Dan Dare (Pilot of the Future)' (Elton John, Bernie Taupin)

Dan Dare became an iconic character for science fiction comic readers after first appearing in Britain's *Eagle* comic in 1950. Elton's super-funkified dedication to the pilot of the future eclipsed all on side one of *Rock of the Westies*, except perhaps for the difficult act to follow that was 'I Feel Like a Bullet (In the Gun of Robert Ford)'.

Elton wanted 'Dan Dare' issued as the first single, and a fine success it could have been too, considering that in 1975 the character Dan Dare was still in the culture, at least for children. Kids were exposed to radio a lot then too, so the single could have worked, especially considering the track's inclusion of Davey Johnstone's robotic-sounding guitar talkbox. This may have been a Joe Walsh influence. Elton's new bassist Kenny Passarelli had a history with Walsh, not to mention being co-writer on the original talkbox vehicle, Walsh's hit 'Rocky Mountain Way'. 'Dan Dare (Pilot of the Future)' was given the prominent album position of side one, track two, released just a few months prior to Peter Frampton exposing the talkbox gimmick to millions via hit live singles like 'Show Me the Way' and the talkbox tour-de-force, 'Do You Feel Like We Do'. 'Dan Dare' could have used that as leverage for a possible successful single, but it wasn't to be.

The concept of the space pilot was well-reflected in the production of 'Dan Dare'. The choruses dropped back to a mellow and trippy combination of synthesizer and backward reverberation effects which placed the listener quite believably off-planet. But it was the chosen first single, 'Island Girl', that would rocket to the top of the US charts.

'Island Girl' (Elton John, Bernie Taupin)
Released as a single A-side, 19 September 1975 (UK), 29 September 1975 (US), b/w 'Sugar on the Floor'. UK: 14. US: 1. CAN: 4. AUS: 12. NZ: 4.

It's a remarkable feat taking this daring lambast of a fictional New York-based streetwalker and channelling it into the catchiest number one this side of the blackest stump you could think of. The fast and frantic pace helped the lyrics escape from Elton's mouth virtually unnoticed - great swathes of the public blissfully ignorant to exactly what was being said. The single was so successful it even kicked Elton's own duet with Neil Sedaka, 'Bad Blood', off the top spot in America. Additionally, 'Island Girl' exposed millions to James Newton-Howard's stunning synthesizer work for the first time.

The overall success of 'Island Girl' stands as an example from a time when the public at large took songs at face value, celebrating what they saw as positive attributes and ignoring the rest. Twentieth-century consumers knew that artful renderings were harmless. The whole music censorship debacle was still virtually a decade away.

'Grow Some Funk of Your Own' (Elton John, Bernie Taupin, Davey Johnstone)
Released as a single double A-side, 9 January 1976 (UK), 12 January 1976 (US), b/w 'I Feel Like a Bullet (In the Gun of Robert Ford)'. CAN: 8. NZ: 39.

The second single's lyric makes more sense when you realise it's someone relaying a dream they had, which was a clever technique that created a layer of protection from those that may have chosen to misinterpret the lyric's Mexican slang. Perceived as a flop, the song actually reached number 8 in Canada. In the USA, where the single sides were flipped, 'I Feel Like a Bullet' peaked at a respectable 14. Nothing to sneeze at.

The band, of course, were in top snappy form, a highlight being Ray Cooper's integrated vibraphone solo, but considering the high level of material in this band's recorded repertoire, 'Grow Some Funk of Your Own' probably belongs in the lower reaches of the list.

'I Feel Like a Bullet (In the Gun of Robert Ford)' (Elton John, Bernie Taupin)
Released as a double A-side single, 9 January 1976 (UK), 12 January 1976 (US), b/w 'Grow Some Funk of Your Own'. US: 14.
Released as a four-song EP, January 1976 (NZ), b/w 'Grow Some Funk of Your Own', 'Pinball Wizard' and 'Ho! Ho! Ho! Who'd Be a Turkey at Christmas'.

Bernie Taupin kept overt sentimentality at bay here, which gave Elton the freedom to bring on the violins metaphorically. With a lyric that stops short of crossing that line, the music will too. So, the resulting ballad was a moving but frank outpouring of a romantic break-up and its aftermath.

The chords did all the work, demonstrating Elton's inspiration from hymns, with their unstable thirds and fifths in the bass providing the emotional undercurrent. If anything else was going to provoke an emotional reaction, it was that soaring Davey Johnstone guitar solo supported by Caleb Quaye's melodic picking accompaniment. This all sounded like a million bucks pouring out of the radio in 1976, being, at least in New Zealand, the side of the single that got the lion's share of airplay. The song was also one of the band's favourites during the recording process.

'Street Kids' (Elton John, Bernie Taupin)

Like a kind of 'Saturday Night's Alright for Fighting, Part 2', 'Street Kids' was a return to the dirty British streets that populated parts of *Goodbye Yellow Brick Road*. You could probably even believably slip this into that album, and it would feel like it belongs. But with cliché-like statements such as 'Squealers can't be trusted' and 'Beggars can't be choosers', the lyric came across as a bit stale compared to those on the above-mentioned double album. But this rock outing did have Elton's repeating speedy and ornate descending chordal piano arpeggio that any rock pianist worth his salt would have to contemplate more than once before replicating accurately.

'Hard Luck Story' (Elton John, Bernie Taupin)

Written for British singer Kiki Dee and released as a fairly mellow single by her a year prior, Elton and band took a slightly harder and more up-tempo approach here, giving the song more street-cred. Much life was also added thanks to drummer Roger Pope's snappy and energetic performance.

One passing passage at the end of each verse was lengthened to fit Elton's particular interpretation, but otherwise, the song was intact. Even so, it's an interesting example of how two versions of the same song can be so similar and yet so different. The song was published under the pseudonyms Ann Orson and Carte Blanche (as in 'orse an' cart).

'Feed Me' (Elton John, Bernie Taupin)

Buried towards the end of side two was a strong piece sharing lyrical themes with 'Have Mercy on the Criminal'. The story's protagonist is running from *something* he's done and is haunted by. Musically, Elton was here moving pretty close to the then-burgeoning West Coast smooth R&B sound. The band was remarkable, and with the track being one of the three retaining the original fretless bass part (see the album introduction above), you get a real sonic picture of the entire group laying it down together.

Other sonic pleasures were present, like the simultaneous rings of James Newton-Howard's Fender Rhodes piano with Ray Cooper's vibes in the introduction. Caleb Quaye's rhythmic bent-string chord accents leading into verse two were another innovative touch. Listening now, I could swear that's Davey Johnstone, Dee Murray and Nigel Olsson on the backing vocals, with that familiar edgy timbre, but it was Johnstone, Kenny Passarelli and Kiki Dee.

'Billy Bones and the White Bird' (Elton John, Bernie Taupin)
Predominantly based on the Bo Diddley beat as heard in the 1958 Johnny Otis hit, 'Willie and the Hand Jive', this cryptic hybrid of sea-tale and pop anthem sat a little uncomfortably among the other tracks. It ended proceedings with a bluster the song never really justified, but it was the obvious closer, ending with a bang. But as if the exceptionally satisfying *Rock of the Westies* wasn't enough, the greatest work from this humongous band was still to come.

Contemporary Tracks:
'Sugar on the Floor' (Kiki Dee)
Released as a single B-side, 19 September 1975 (UK), 29 September 1975 (US), b/w 'Island Girl'.
Kiki Dee's 1973 Rocket Records album Loving and Free (produced by Elton and Clive Franks) housed the original recording of her song 'Sugar on the Floor'. But an unassuming band arrangement blurred the song's emotional power. Elton's recording brought it fully to life with just vocal and piano. Clearly, he loved it, going by the level of commitment given to this fine performance.

Having your song ride along on the B-side of a huge hit like 'Island Girl' was a painless privilege reserved for a few. So, although Kiki and Elton's coming duet 'Don't Go Breaking My Heart' became a monster international hit, it was a John/Taupin composition after all, which means 'Sugar on the Floor' must certainly be Kiki Dee's most successful composition.

'Planes' (Elton John, Bernie Taupin)
Released on *Rare Masters* compilation, 31 December 1993 (UK), 20 October 1992 (US).
This odd acoustic outtake with incongruous synthesizer bass was eventually released on the 1992 *Rare Masters* compilation and again on the 1996 *Rock of the Westies* Rocket reissue. It seemed to refer to a longing for fame and success while being stuck in a job. The Casbah mentioned presumably refers to the '60s London strip joint and not the Liverpool club where the Beatles played early gigs. This possibly dates the seemingly autobiographical lyric back to the *Captain Fantastic* days, though realistically it doesn't come close to the strength of that material.

Elton's version of 'Planes' was little more than a demo, so the song is best experienced from the fuller version by Zombies vocalist Colin Blunstone, issued on his 1977 *Planes* album.

Here and There (Live) (1976)

Personnel:
Elton John, John Lennon: vocals, piano
Lesley Duncan, Davey Johnstone, Dee Murray, Nigel Olsson: backing vocals
Dee Murray: bass
Nigel Olsson: drums
Davey Johnstone, John Lennon: guitars
The Muscle Shoals Horns: horn section
Ray Cooper: percussion
Recorded: 18 May 1974, Royal Festival Hall, London & 28 November 1974, Madison Square Garden, New York
Producer: Gus Dudgeon
Engineers: Gus Dudgeon, Phil Dunne
Release date: 30 April 1976 (UK). 3 May 1976 (US)
Chart placings: UK: 6, US: 4, CAN: 13, NZ: 3

Here and There was Elton's final contractual obligation to DJM Records. The material was taken from two concerts with side one from the Saturday 18 May 1974 Invalid Children's Aid Society Benefit at London's Royal Festival Hall in the presence of Her Royal Highness, Princess Margaret.

After opening intro music of 'God Save the Queen', Elton presented the music chronologically, starting with a solo 'Skyline Pigeon'. Dee Murray and Nigel Olsson then joined in for several numbers including 'Love Song' with its writer and concert guest, Lesley Duncan. Guitarist Davey Johnstone and percussionist Ray Cooper were added from 'Honky Cat' onwards. The original vinyl album misplaced 'Love Song' in the chronology.

Side two came from the Madison Square Garden Thanksgiving concert on Thursday 28 November 1974, the very night Elton and band were joined onstage by John Lennon.

Lennon's three songs were omitted from the original vinyl edition of *Here and There*, but in this instance, we'll examine the entire album track-listing as sequenced on the 1995 Mercury and 1996 Rocket reissues, which were remixed by Gus Dudgeon.

Here and There went gold in America within a month of release. It was also distinguished by the fact that it was the last release to feature this band line-up until their reconciliation for 1983's *Too Low For Zero*, seven years after the live album release, but nine years after its recording.

'Skyline Pigeon' (Elton John, Bernie Taupin)

After a short introduction where Elton said, 'I just have to take me ring off', the 'Here' side of the album live at London's Royal Festival Hall, began with 'Skyline Pigeon' solo at the piano. With the high end of his vocal range in effortless flight, his delivery was virtually identical to the recent recording issued as the B-side of 'Daniel', though marred by one or two throat flubs towards the end. With three recordings of this number now available at the release of *Here and There*, I'd point you towards the 'Daniel' B-side as the definitive version, although the original inception on *Empty Sky* might be more satisfactory and representative to chronology buffs.

'Border Song' (Elton John, Bernie Taupin)

This performance is fascinating in comparison to the three-piece live version from the *17-11-70* concert four years earlier. That performance was edgy and aggressive, with Elton even sounding angry in his delivery - you could hear the hunger in it. On this newer performance, we had the same band (plus Davey Johnstone and Ray Cooper), multiple hit records and 314 concerts down the track, giving a perfectly tight and glossy performance. It was still funky like its live predecessor, but the desperation was gone.

'Take Me to the Pilot' (Elton John, Bernie Taupin)

Here the band gave an accomplished and effortless treat, as tightened up by three years of virtually relentless touring. The second half of the guitar solo is emphasised by a pitch-shifter effect on the right side of the stereo spectrum, which I suspect was added by Gus Dudgeon at the time of remixing.

'Country Comfort' (Elton John, Bernie Taupin)

More laid back than the *Tumbleweed Connection* version, it feels slower but actually isn't. The highlight is Davey Johnstone's gorgeous guitar solo marked by tasteful slow volume attacks with a tone resembling his moves on 'I've Seen That Movie Too' or Kiki Dee's 1973 Rocket Records single, 'Amoureuse'.

'Love Song' (Lesley Duncan)

Released as a single A-side (Edited), April 1976 (US and CAN), b/w 'Love Song (Long version)'. US: 18 (AC). CAN: 85.
Released as a single A-side, 1976 (NZ), b/w 'Skyline Pigeon (Live)'.
After introducing Lesley Duncan, Elton and band launched into what I'd call the definitive version of 'Love Song'. This performance had a musical momentum it lacked on both *Tumbleweed Connection* and Lesley Duncan's original version but was smoothed by a poppy kind of mid-'70s AM-radio cream that was nearing the end of its days. The track was issued as a promotional single, but despite generous airplay, failed to chart. But it did earn top twenty status in some American states.

'Bad Side of the Moon' (Elton John, Bernie Taupin)

An accomplished bluesy guitar introduction a la The Allman Brothers ushered in the piano, while accents from Ray Cooper's tubular bells hinted towards Elton and band's soon-to-be-recorded cover of the Beatles' 'Lucy in the Sky with Diamonds'. It all unleashed a totally new and contemporary sounding version of the original 'Border Song' B-side.

'Burn Down the Mission' (Elton John, Bernie Taupin)

This performance of the *Tumbleweed Connection* climax began fairly predictably, but the choruses revealed the welcome emphasis of arranged melodic touches, clearly developed over so many live performances. This was a fairly frantic version where Elton attempted to enliven the audience in the central section, obviously realising pretty quickly that a piano solo was in order to accompany what amounted to polite clapping and possibly jewellery-rattling.

'Honky Cat' (Elton John, Bernie Taupin)

Sounding as fresh as the day it was first recorded, 'Honky Cat' was nevertheless taken advantage of a little in this instance. The second half made a mockery to an extent. The hokey references to Dixie tunes were belittling to the current number. Unfortunately too, Ray Cooper's lengthy duck call solo, though not without ability, reduced the song to mere music hall entertainment, as if the audience were going to be a hard sell (the single did only reach number 31 in the UK after all). I'd wager that Elton loved the musical highlights here, of which there were a few, but disliked the need for forced entertainment.

'Crocodile Rock' (Elton John, Bernie Taupin)

As to be expected - virtually identical to the studio version but less interesting. Of interest is the additional organ played by percussionist Ray Cooper.

'Candle in the Wind' (Elton John, Bernie Taupin)

For some reason, Elton exchanges the word 'grace' for the word 'strength' in the first verse and its later repeat. Today the entire performance sounds like a catching of the breath after the earlier frenzies, presuming that the songs included in the remixed and expanded edition of *Here and There* were in identical sequence to the concert. But the backing vocals are performed as a perfect likeness to the studio version, regardless of Davey Johnstone neglecting his harmony in the title lines to contend with that prominent guitar lick he wasn't convinced by in the first place.

'Your Song' (Elton John, Bernie Taupin)

The song often dedicated to the audience was here tackled solo at the piano. Elton's voice was perfect in this period, conditioned through multiple performances across lengthy tours. This may even be the finest recorded execution of this standard.

'Saturday Night's Alright for Fighting' (Elton John, Bernie Taupin)

Elton managed to extract some singing from the audience in the extended play-out section of what was otherwise a dead ringer for the studio take.

'Funeral for a Friend/Love Lies Bleeding' (Elton John, Bernie Taupin)

Side two was the New York or 'There' side of the album. Beginning with David Hentschel's recorded synthesizer introduction, played directly from *Goodbye Yellow Brick Road*, the band here laid out a sterling and energetic take. Key synthesizer parts were, of course, absent from the bulk of the performance, but it was more than made up for with veracity. A highlight at the entry of verse two was Dee Murray and Davey Johnstone's tantalising dual variation on the bass line. The band had toured this material throughout the Pacific, and North America for the bulk of 1974 and moves like that would keep the material fresh. They were tight, and it showed.

'Rocket Man' (Elton John, Bernie Taupin)

A fine rendition indeed. You'd swear it was the studio recording for most of it. Variation appeared in the form of Davey Johnstone's slide guitar lines which took a few extra leaps skyward in this performance. In the absence of the verse two synthesizer parts, Dee Murray improvised in the upper register of the bass which gave an extra level of lift-off and a floating texture appropriate to the concept and not unlike the liquid moves that he would develop for later Elton ballads like 'Blue Eyes' and 'Cold as Christmas'.

'Take Me to the Pilot' (Elton John, Bernie Taupin)

The piano moves that only Elton could make, and that in the early days caused any piano he played to sound like him, were all over this protracted gospel introduction. Throw in sprinkles of Randy Newman-esque chord turnarounds and a sudden blues vocal howl that briefly traded licks with Davey's guitar, and the song kicked in proper.

There was much more spring in the band's step here than in the above Royal Festival Hall version. However, functioning as the original vinyl album closer, the track was an anti-climax. But this song and the following 'Bennie and the Jets', though in reverse order on the vinyl, were only the third and fourth songs of a concert that had yet to heat up. The atmosphere would have been palpable knowing you were about to spring John Lennon on your audience.

'Bennie and the Jets' (Elton John, Bernie Taupin)

Minus all the production tricks that buried the rhythm section on the studio version, 'Bennie and the Jets' benefits here by being funkier and more in your face. The R&B foundation that qualified the single for *Soul Train* inclusion is plain to hear. Dee Murray's fallback funk signature would come more to the fore on '80s Elton albums like *Jump Up* and *Too Low for Zero*, but that side of his contribution always shone in live performances, this being a perfect example.

'Grey Seal' (Elton John, Bernie Taupin)

Taken slightly faster than the studio version, this performance exudes energy, but it does lose vitality through the end section by continuing to be played as a straight four rhythm as opposed to the constant snare drum accents of the studio version. The ending is made interesting by intermittent rhythmic accents beneath a repeated and flowing Celtic-sounding guitar line recalling British folk outfits like Pentangle and Steeleye Span - a dynamic and unexpected touch.

'Daniel' (Elton John, Bernie Taupin)

Announced in advance only as a favourite of Elton's, the introductory rock and roll piano vamp fools you into thinking you're about to hear anything but the mellow 1973 hit. Extra vigour is supplied by the grand piano standing in for the Fender Rhodes electric heard on the record, and by Davey's electric rhythm flourishes as an understudy for those of the record's acoustic guitars. The roof caves in slightly with the solo lacking the personality of the studio version's synthesizer, here replaced by clean and unassuming guitar, but for those that might have considered the studio version to be a bit on the slow-boil, this version is more rounded and satisfying.

'You're So Static' (Elton John, Bernie Taupin)

After an introductory announcement, the band plays a brief instrumental funk vamp to accompany the Muscle Shoals Horns to the stage. What follows is a version even more frantic than that on *Caribou*, but with an identical horn arrangement, minus the high solo lines.

'Whatever Gets You Thru the Night' (John Lennon)

Coming as a complete surprise to the audience, John Lennon was introduced, walking on to rapturous applause. Here he kept his end of the agreement to appear live with Elton if 'Whatever Gets You Thru the Night' hit the top of the charts, which it just had in America on 16 November 1974. This live recording is a near identical replica of the single.

'Lucy in the Sky with Diamonds' (John Lennon, Paul McCartney)

'Lucy in the Sky' was performed here identically to Elton's then-current single version, even down to the tubular bell touches. The only additions were a complimentary horn arrangement and John Lennon singing part of the central reggae chorus, solo.

'I Saw Her Standing There' (John Lennon, Paul McCartney)

Sung originally by Paul McCartney, Lennon and Elton here sang this Beatles classic in unison. Lennon's rhythm guitar playing was flawless, and Davey

Johnstone complimented the first verse by incorporating The Beatles' 'I Feel Fine' guitar riff.

'Don't Let the Sun Go Down on Me' (Elton John, Bernie Taupin)

A respectable version indeed, but it lacked the thick and creamy backing vocals of the studio version.

'Your Song' (Elton John, Bernie Taupin)

Accompanied at first by bassist Dee Murray, the addition of the full band from verse two onwards hauled the classic ballad into the current 1974 vibe of Elton's work, updating it for the better. If this vocal had been as flawless as on the above Royal Festival Hall version, we'd really have something. Not that the singing suffered - Elton made some fine vocal variations in the final choruses, higher and more urgent than the original, further complimenting what was still a very popular song.

'The Bitch Is Back' (Elton John, Bernie Taupin)

The *Caribou* album opener functioned here as concert closer, taken quite fast, abandoning any feel the original may have had. But every concert needs something like this, and now 'Saturday Night's Alright for Fighting' had some stiff competition for the manic finale.

For the 1995 remix, an audio effect of rich stereo chorus was added to the bass, colouring it tastefully, if unnecessarily for such a fast number.

Blue Moves (1976)

Personnel:
Elton John: vocals, piano, electric harpsichord, harmonium
Carl Fortina: accordion
Curt Becher, Cindy Bullens, Clark Burroughs, Joe Chemay, David Crosby, Ron Hicklin, Bruce Johnston, Jon Joyce, Gene Morford, Graham Nash, Toni Tenille: backing vocals
Kenny Passarelli: bass
Michael Hurwitz: cello solo
Roger Pope: drums
Davey Johnstone, Caleb Quaye: guitars, dulcimer, mandolin, sitar
Michael Brecker, Randy Brecker, Barry Rogers, David Sanborn: horn section
James Newton-Howard: keyboards, organ
Ray Cooper: percussion, glockenspiel, marimba, tubular bells, vibes
Choir: The Cornerstone Institutional Baptist and Southern Californian Community directed by Rev. James Cleveland
Orchestras: The London Symphony Orchestra, The Martyn Ford Orchestra, The Gene Page Strings
Recorded: March 1976 at Eastern Sound, Toronto; EMI, Abbey Road, London; Brother Studio, Santa Monica; Sunset Sound, Los Angeles
Producer: Gus Dudgeon
Engineers: Gus Dudgeon, Mark Howlett, John Kurlander, Earl Mankey, John Stewart
Arrangers: Curt Becher (Vocals), Paul Buckmaster, Daryl Dragon (Vocals), Bruce Johnston (Vocals), James Newton-Howard
Release date: 30 April 1976 (UK), 3 May 1976 (US)
Chart placings: UK: 3, US: 3, CAN: 4, AUS: 8

March 1976 saw Elton and band uproot to a fresh recording location at Eastern Sound in Toronto, Canada. It was a complete contrast to the Caribou Ranch, and the music too saw a stylistic departure. The rock-focused numbers that populated *Rock of the Westies* now opened out into a more liquid and at times sombre, but adventurous and eclectic collection.

Still wanting to record more as a band unit than as Elton and backing band, the musicians dug their heels in, breaking it to producer Gus Dudgeon that there would be no going back to re-record parts of the basic tracks. Overdubs would be vocals, horn section and orchestra, but the rest would be what came from the band live off the studio floor. Having said that, overdubs were plenty, as were personnel - *Blue Moves* boasting the largest cast of musicians since *Madman Across the Water*.

Fitting the band-as-a-unit concept, various members contributed to the writing. In fact, many of these songs were written during the recording of the previous album, and now some of those collaborations came to light. Enough material was produced to ensure a double album. Some experimentation occurred, including three instrumentals - one of which, 'Your Starter For...', was a Caleb Quaye composition. The sessions also hatched the basic track for the Elton and Kiki Dee duet 'Don't Go Breaking My Heart'. Deciding it didn't fit the vibe of the album, Elton made other plans for the sprightly Tamla Motown tribute.

Tired of his image being required for record covers, Elton took an about-turn with the album artwork, using a pre-existing painting he owned titled 'The Guardian Readers', by British artist Patrick Proctor.

More about-turns ensued, the least of which wasn't that *Blue Moves* was the first Elton album released through his own Rocket Records label outside of the USA. He also broke his agreement with Caleb Quaye by busting out 'Crocodile Rock' at what ended up as the band's final concert at Madison Square Garden on Tuesday 17 August 1976. Elton felt he was peaking and needed some time out. Not long after, producer Gus Dudgeon made his departure from the fold, not for personal reasons, but over a political matter concerning Rocket Records. Gus stood up at a board meeting one day and just said 'That's it, I'm off.' - abandoning his directorship in the process.

Elton has said that the hit albums had been piling up for so long that there was now a feeling of 'How many times can we do this?' So he made the album for himself. Commercial considerations were not at the forefront this time, and certain personal tensions on the part of many concerned contributed to the material.

But the album became a success. *Blue Moves* went gold upon its October 1976 release, then expanding to Elton's first official platinum sales achievement in December - platinum certifications not having existed prior to 1976. He has always claimed that *Blue Moves* is his favourite.

'Your Starter For...' (Caleb Quaye)

At a certain point in proceedings, it became clear that an introductory piece was required to start the album off. Guitarist Caleb Quaye had a little practice piece he used to play around with sometimes, so he played it for the band, and they jumped on it.

Simple on the surface, the little intro was deceptively complex and unconventional. It was one minute and 23 seconds of subtle album-opener that led so perfectly into the following track, 'Tonight', that the two sounded made for each other, though they couldn't have been more stylistically different. It was certainly an adventurous tie-in of two disparate pieces.

'One Horse Town', with its quiet entry and moody electric piano leading into that tense guitar riff with the band at full tilt, could have also made an impressive, if more dramatic, album-opener. But what sense would there have been in going anywhere near competing with the tension that characterised the introduction of the former double album, *Goodbye Yellow Brick Road*?

What we ended up with was 'Your Starter For...' - a piece that is unique in Elton's recorded repertoire for appearing to be the only track he didn't write or even perform on. He was credited with piano in the liner notes, but the bulk of the instrumentation was guitar, mandolin, vibes and synthesizer. Listening to the song today, piano is not evident in the mix at all, even with the centre channel removed, which always brings out details and reveals parts you've never noticed before. At 1m:03s I struggled to hear what I thought was one high piano chord, but I can't confirm its existence. When talking to *Blue Moves* bassist Kenny Passarelli, I brought this up. Playing the track on his end of the phone, he too was unable to identify the existence of any piano in the mix. Therefore, we can safely assume Elton is not on the track in any way – the perfect contrast to the other double-album opener.

'Tonight' (Elton John, Bernie Taupin)

Clearly considered an important track, important enough to hold back the dynamic 'One Horse Town' until track three, 'Tonight' added another moving ballad to the repertoire, but one that was dark and foreboding. The credit for the mood created here must surely go to arranger James Newton-Howard. It was being involved with Elton John that brought Newton-Howards orchestration skills to the table, originally on the Kiki Dee duet, 'Don't Go Breaking My Heart'.

It's mind-boggling to contemplate the 24-year-old Newton-Howard, who after getting the big gig in the first place, was then through the recording of *Blue Moves*, given the opportunity to arrange for and conduct not one but two orchestras, one of them the London Symphony Orchestra no less. Like Gus Dudgeon jested in a 1973 interview, start at the top and work your way down.

So here was Newton-Howard at the helm of the LSO, and recording at Abbey Road Studio 2 to boot, the location of the majority of The Beatles' recordings. The piano track and a guide vocal were pre-existing, recorded back in Toronto at Eastern Sound. But the issue was going to be keeping the orchestra in time with the recorded piano, to meet all the cues correctly. It was like a test of a sort. Usually, the piano might go down along with the orchestra, with everyone in the same room watching the conductor, which made things much easier. Newton-Howard would have had to familiarise himself closely enough with Elton's piano performance to be aware of every little variation in speed and dynamic in order to make the addition of orchestra as seamless as possible.

This snag would have challenged even the most seasoned conductor, and it's a credit to the young Newton-Howard that he successfully met the challenge. But it's interesting to listen now and try to perceive the more than 5000-mile distance between that piano and that orchestra.

'One Horse Town' (Elton John, Bernie Taupin, James Newton-Howard)

For all its emotional depth, the lengthy 'Tonight' seemed like more introductory music coming before 'One Horse Town', which is where things really started to move with it the closest thing to an all-out rock song on *Blue Moves*.

Instrumentally, the guitars took the lead, the modulating introduction riff giving a subtle but undeniable taste of instability. Guitarist Caleb Quaye stole the show with the coup de grace of a double-verse-length solo that matched the track's vitality by speaking faster than it could think, and in more than one instance was interrupted by Davey Johnstone's slide guitar interjections.

There were lyrical nods to the Americana of the past here too with lines like 'Half a mile of Alabama mud bed ground' and 'If you want to hear Susanna, Then they'll pick all night'. The popular 1800s Stephen Foster standard 'Oh! Susanna' cast quite a shadow considering its famous opening line, 'I come from Alabama with a banjo on my knee' influenced this rock song nearly 130 years later.

A further influence here was the return of arranger Paul Buckmaster, whose last contribution had been to 'Have Mercy on the Criminal' from *Don't Shoot Me I'm Only the Piano Player*. His ability to make an already exemplary song outstanding by casting a darkly positive tone over proceedings had not faltered one iota. It gave 'One Horse Town' a depth, providing a sub-plot to the lyric. The narrator's need to escape from this safe, innocent and bland place is clear, but his naivety is betrayed by the orchestra's exposition of a gritty underbelly already hinted at by the intro guitar riff. The foundation of manic rhythmic energy is tamed by Buckmaster's ominous subterrane in a manner resembling the unavoidable truths he splotched onto the 'Sixty Years On' canvas. But the blood that seeped down that wall now reverses back up on the final landing chord of 'One Horse Town', where it slowly inches toward the top, and the bubble silently pops.

'Chameleon' (Elton John, Bernie Taupin)
Released as a single B-side, 4 February 1977 (UK and NZ), b/w 'Crazy Water'.
The tried and true descending five-chord sequence first offered in 'The Greatest Discovery', repeated more than once in 'Son of Your Father' and made infamous in the introduction to 'Goodbye Yellow Brick Road', now made another undisguised appearance. Not that it matters – the romantic composers had used the sequence multiple times, and anyone that wants to split these kinds of musical hairs has probably never heard any two blues songs back to back.

The chord sequence is also heard in the Beach Boys' 1970 song 'Forever', so as a compositional device it was clearly still up for grabs. In fact, after being asked to write a song for the Beach Boys, Elton and Bernie wrote the ballad 'Chameleon' specifically for them. It's not stylistically unlike the material from the Beach Boys 1973 post-Brian Wilson epic, *Holland*. Elton worked hard on the song, claiming it took six months to write, finally finishing it on a break in Hawaii.

After all that, the Beach Boys turned it down. But in recording it for *Blue Moves*, the song was slightly anointed with the surf magic when Beach Boy Bruce Johnston arranged and sang in the backing vocal group, so the song finally earned its stripes. Furthermore, *Blue Moves* bassist Kenny Passarelli, after having worked with everyone from Joe Walsh to Dan Fogelberg and Stephen Stills, claims 'Chameleon' to be his favourite of the recordings to which he's contributed.

'Boogie Pilgrim' (Elton John, Bernie Taupin, Davey Johnstone, Caleb Quaye)

After performing 'Bennie and the Jets' on *Soul Train* in 1975 and gaining the respect that came from having a top twenty hit on the *Billboard Hot Soul Singles* chart, Elton had every reason to be confident should he choose to work in that field. Not that he was always that calculating - the music would generally come out how it came out unless it was a specific style homage such as 'Philadelphia Freedom'.

The *Caribou* album had hinted at soul by featuring the Tower of Power horn section, but none of that material really approached the style except for a whiff of it in 'You're So Static' and a bigger slice in the B-side 'Sick City'. 'Dan Dare (Pilot of the Future)' from *Rock of the Westies* had headed more definitively in a funk direction but had been tamed by a rock edge. So not to do it by halves, 'Boogie Pilgrim' plunged into the funk/soul waters once and for all. Of course, having the band more involved in the inception of certain songs probably had a lot to do with the stylistic element, and both Davey Johnstone and Caleb Quaye had a writing credit on this song.

Complimenting the stonkin' rhythm section was a horn section featuring the cream of the crop - Michael Brecker, Randy Brecker and David Sanborn - who provided smooth chords, sharp accents and signature unidirectional arpeggio stabs in the play-out section. Davey Johnstone kept things raw by sawing off a searing slide guitar solo to top it all off.

The lyrics, though hinting at a kind of street politics, kept things light with a fun, almost sing-along chorus that was punctuated by a gospel choir on the title lines. Mission accomplished.

'Cage the Songbird' (Elton John, Bernie Taupin, Davey Johnstone)

Perhaps the most poignant song in this collection, the acoustic 'Cage the Songbird' is purported to be a fictional reimagining of the death of French chanteuse Edith Piaf, aka the Little Sparrow. Her life was dramatic and eventful enough without inventing a suicide to emblazon it even further, but it was precisely that aspect that gave the song its power. Without that, it would be more stonewall tribute than story. Of course, the lyric never once mentioned her name and Bernie very well could have been alluding more to a concept than a specific individual - like in 'Candle in the Wind', despite the name the famous lament dropped.

In a move that was unusual for an Elton track, the vocals were taken in three-part harmony, virtually all the way through - sparkling due to the inclusion of singers David Crosby and Graham Nash. If anyone was going to do three-part vocals, they were the guys you wanted backing you up.

In 1976, 'Cage the Songbird' was covered by Kiki Dee in a similarly acoustic rendition adorned by a dramatic string arrangement. Sadly, her *Cage the Songbird* album was inexplicably shelved immediately post-'Don't Go Breaking My Heart', leaving a gaping hole that the album could have successfully filled. But, in at least one published interview, she made no secret of her distaste for fame, which may have played a part. The album was eventually released in 2008.

'Crazy Water' (Elton John, Bernie Taupin)

Released as a single A-side, 4 February 1977 (UK and NZ), b/w 'Chameleon'. UK: 27. Released as a single B-side, 14 March 1977 (AUS), b/w 'Bite Your Lip (Get Up and Dance)'.

The album's third single was a big old metaphor for the abyss that can form between two individuals – In this case referring to Bernie's marriage, according to some. It was a sweeping storm of a track, thanks to arranger Paul Buckmaster's flurry of overcast string lines floating fast above drummer Roger Pope's spirited drum rhythm. Keyboardist James Newton-Howard took a cue from Stevie Wonder with double clavinets pounding out their monophonic lines, topped with a coating of backing vocals arranged by Daryl Dragon of the Captain and Tennille.

The single went unissued in the USA where they had the 'Bite Your Lip' single to contend with at the time. Considering 'Crazy Water' was only a moderate chart success, we can be thankful that charts have never been a measure of actual musical merit. But when producer Gus Dudgeon has gone on record as saying 'Crazy Water' is one of Elton's greatest tracks, you can more reliably take that to the bank.

'Shoulder Holster' (Elton John, Bernie Taupin)

Released as a single B-side, 10 October 1976 (UK), 1 November 1976 (US), b/w 'Sorry Seems to Be the Hardest Word'.

Bernie referenced Americana once again in this story that took inspiration from two traditional American popular songs based on real-life events; 'Frankie and Johnny' and 'Stagger Lee'. The former was the true story of Frankie Baker, who in St. Louis, Missouri, 1899, shot her lover upon finding him with someone else. She claimed to have done so in self-defence after he came at her with a knife. Frankie was acquitted, though is executed in some versions of the song, of which there are many. 'Stagger Lee' was based on Lee Shelton, a St. Louis pimp who on Christmas Eve 1895 got into a bar dispute with a rival underworld figure, shooting him dead. Shelton was tried and convicted of murder. Both songs appeared in the culture as if they'd always been there and original authorship was difficult to determine. In line with folk song traditions, many versions were given lyric variations. Elton's funky horn-section-driven tale 'Shoulder Holster' stops short of tragedy after the character Dolly Summers takes a gun in pursuit of her unfaithful other half, but at the last minute decides against firing.

The recording was piano-dominant, minus guitar except for bass, the play-out section enhanced by a signature solo from renowned American saxophonist, David Sanborn. This brought the first disc of *Blue Moves* to a close on a high note, both musical and figurative.

'Sorry Seems to Be the Hardest Word' (Elton John, Bernie Taupin)

Released as a single A-side, 10 October 1976 (UK), 1 November 1976 (US), b/w 'Shoulder Holster'. UK: 11. US: 6. CAN: 3. AUS: 19. NZ: 7.

As alluded to in the discussion of 'Don't Let the Sun Go Down on Me' and its characteristics, 'Sorry Seems To Be the Hardest Word' is the sound of Elton John crossing a line that signified a shift towards more commercial considerations, whether it was conscious or not. But issuing his music from this point on his own Rocket Records label probably had something to do with it.

The song was clearly standard quality, attracting cover versions from the outset. American soul singer Walter Jackson's 1977 easy-listening orchestral version was followed a year later by jazz vocalist Dee Dee Bridgewater's howling, and dynamic R&B take, which demonstrated the potential for a well-written song to be taken in virtually any direction.

Over the years, everyone from Ray Charles, Barry Manilow and Shirley Bassey, to Elaine Page, Diana Krall and Mary J. Blige have had a stab at the romantic ballad. So whatever decision Elton was making by releasing this single, clearly it was the right one. The song was a top 20 hit everywhere and was certified a gold single in January 1977.

Everything was about to change generally in music anyway, and Elton would make more changes too. *Blue Moves* would be the last album with lyrics entirely written by Bernie until 1983's *Too Low for Zero*. Another recent change had seen Elton contribute more song titles, and in some cases, parts of lyrics. This very song's opening line, 'What have I got to do to make you love me?', came to Elton as he formulated the chords beneath it.

'Out of the Blue' (Elton John, Bernie Taupin)

This experimental instrumental was representative of the jazz/fusion movement that was exploding at the time or was at least as representative of it as you'll find on any Elton John record. Not dissimilar to the British end of that field, it also came uncannily close to a Frank Zappa style in the accented section towards the end, thanks to Ray Cooper's vibes getting in on the act.

Oddly credited to Elton and Bernie, the piece actually came about from the band jamming, so it's the one *Blue Moves* composition that should be credited to the entire band. It is quite a melodically elaborate composition to come out of a jam, but these were some pretty heavy musos who could turn their hand to anything. I use the word 'jam' in the old parlance, meaning a band improvising a new composition on the spot. The piece clearly underwent an amount of arrangement before finding its final form, but it still could have been written and recorded in the same session. True or not, this and all of the *Blue Moves* instrumentals were a breath of fresh air from an artist who'd done it all and was willing to find even more stuff to do.

'Between Seventeen and Twenty' (Elton John, Bernie Taupin, Davey Johnstone, Caleb Quaye)

According to certain sources, this song was just the latest in a series that Bernie wrote about his then-wife Maxine – a line that started back in 1971 with 'Tiny Dancer'. It's not the purpose of this book to dwell too much on the whys and wherefores of personal matters pertaining to the songs, suffice it to say that this was probably one of the *most* personal.

The track had an American sound that seemed to take influence from a specific country/funk/rock style that was prevalent at the time in the music of artists like the Byrds' Gene Clark and Stephen Stills. Take into account Bruce Johnston's expressly Beach Boys-inflected backing vocal arrangement, and you had another perfect slice of cultural Americana, now updated from the 1870s to the 1970s.

'The Wide-Eyed and Laughing' (Elton John, Bernie Taupin, Davey Johnstone, James Newton-Howard, Caleb Quaye)

Another style fairly unique to Elton's repertoire was delivered here. This was an out-'n'-out psychedelic-folk gem replete with sitars. Eerie synthesizers also weaved their way through to remind us what decade it actually was. Certain earlier Elton songs had flirted with psychedelia, lyrically at the beginning of the John/Taupin collaboration, and later instrumentally, such as in the backwards guitar effects of 'I've Seen That Movie Too' and the space rock audio imagery of 'I've Seen the Saucers'. At least in effect, 'The Wide-Eyed and Laughing' was Elton's first and probably only overt plunge into the genre, its acoustic foundation not unlike early T. Rex work and its '60s vibe personified by the presence again of singers David Crosby and Graham Nash. There were five writers on the piece too – always an opportunity for endless possibilities, which of course was what the spirit of *Blue Moves* was all about.

'Someone's Final Song' (Elton John, Bernie Taupin)

Side three had been a real grab-bag of styles and influences, not to mention surprises. But now to close the side we were offloaded firmly back into Elton land for the bluest move of all. The lyric, clearly a suicide note, had an interesting structure where the first three lines were an introduction to the note by an impartial narrator and the rest of the lyric was the actual note. Elton seamlessly strung these together where another writer might have predictably sectioned out the three-line introduction in the style of some songs from musicals, which the lyric does seem to cry out for if you read it cold.

This brooding ballad with Elton on acoustic piano and James Newton-Howard on electric piano and synthesizer, bore a similarity to 'Sorry Seems to Be the Hardest Word', 'Tonight', and the following side four opener, 'Where's the Shoorah?'. But 'Someone's Final Song' was *Blue Moves'* darkest corner, despite the tragic true story told in the coming jazz-tinged 'Idol'.

'Where's the Shoorah?' (Elton John, Bernie Taupin)

Firmly a gospel ballad, at least in stylistic approach, intensified thanks to the presence of the Cornerstone Baptist Choir, 'Where's the Shoorah?' went nowhere near the tradition lyrically. However, as mentioned earlier, by 1976 all kinds of taboos had been broken, and borders transgressed when it came to songwriting norms. Purists saw that as blasphemy while others saw it as progression. The song did have a flavour of New Orleans about it which further placed the influence in the American South. But the song was enigmatic, almost like seeing a short movie scene out of context. Avant-garde could be another description, in light of the fact that the song meddled with tradition. On the surface, it could have been heard as just another ballad, but the song left more unanswered questions than the one in the title.

'If There's a God in Heaven (What's He Waiting For?)' (Elton John, Bernie Taupin, Davey Johnstone)

It's a relief to realise that this seeming political statement was written as a joke. Not that it was disturbing or pretentious – it made its point clearly and that was enough. But pain came in the form of some critics casting aspersions purely out of a distaste for political commentary coming from a quarter where there formerly was none, or expecting such commentary to be a Dylan-esque dissertation.

American soul group The Chi-Lites had a track titled 'There Will Never Be Any Peace on Earth (Till God is Seated at the Conference Table)'. Elton suggested to Bernie that they write a song like that but in a really tacky 'big men make millions while children starve' kind of way, to see if they could get away with it and who would take it seriously or not. Of course, it was taken seriously, and no one got the joke.

But they got a fine track out of it that had the band sporting their abundant wares yet again. Rather than being a vehicle for idiosyncratic instrumental passages (with the exception of Caleb Quaye's understated guitar solo), it was more an example of the band excelling at staying out of each other's way. Drums, bass, piano, organ, two guitars and a string section, simultaneous at times, was a lot to have on the plate. No wonder it was decided against adding backing vocals to the mix (figurative).

If anything else stood out, it was Paul Buckmaster's effortless stab at the

Philadelphia string arrangement style, which was equally at home here as his usual darker colourings.

'Idol' (Elton John, Bernie Taupin)

It was possible for multiple subjects to influence a Bernie Taupin lyric, as confirmed with 'Candle in the Wind' when he stated it could as easily have been about actor James Dean or musician Jim Morrison. Multiple influences could have been the case here, too. Taupin was convinced that radio would pick up this song for airplay, but the lyric never stated who the subject was, which could have marred the song's accessibility. It did, however, appear to focus fairly obviously on the career trajectory of Elvis Presley, who was still alive when the song was released, and the song was all the better for it. It could only have suffered if promoted as a post-death tribute the following year.

In another left turn, Elton set the song in a smoky jazz idiom, enhanced by the presence of a horn section coaxing the emotion from the lyrics by subtly reflecting their ups and downs. It's a shame more wasn't made of the short piano solo at 2m:49s, which seemed unsure of itself and was a lost opportunity, but it did fit the fragility of the concept. The mournful track came to a close with saxophonist David Sanborn's urgent and moving solo, effectively having the final say on an album now winding down to its finish.

'Theme from a Non-Existent TV Series' (Elton John, Bernie Taupin)

More than believable as a 1970s TV theme for a spy show or something of that nature, this brief morsel of instrumental music effectively functioned as a showcase for keyboardist James Newton-Howard. Bass and drums notwithstanding, synthesizer and electric piano were the main features, along with Elton's electric harpsichord flourishes and Davey Johnstone's occasional mandolin interjections.

Like the instrumental 'Out of the Blue', this miniature was credited to both Elton and Bernie. His involvement in the instrumental pieces was unlikely though, unless he came up with titles of course, which was always a possibility.

'Bite Your Lip (Get Up and Dance!)' (Elton John, Bernie Taupin)

Released as a single A-side, 3 June 1977 (UK and NZ), b/w 'Chicago' (By Kiki Dee). UK: 28.

Released as a single A-side, 31 January 1977 (US and CAN), b/w 'Chameleon'. US: 28. CAN: 51.

Released as a single A-side, 14 March 1977 (AUS), b/w 'Crazy Water'. AUS: 72.

Perfectly acceptable to close such a mellow double album with, if this second *Blue Moves* single wasn't an outright attempt at a Top 40 hit, it was at least an obvious choice to have a crack at the singles charts with. It was more likely a bit of fun so the band could let off some steam, aided by the outrageous idea

to add a choir and orchestra to it. The Cornerstone Baptist choir had come
down to Sunset Sound in Los Angeles to sing on 'Boogie Pilgrim' and 'Where's
the Shoorah?' anyway, so might as well use them on this party sing-along, right?
Plus, why not get the Gene Page Strings in specially for this one song in order
for James Newton-Howard to work more on his arrangement chops. It made
perfect sense!

But I jest. Fading this virtual seven-minute mammoth three minutes early
for the American single *did* make sense. To be fair, there was really only so
much of the repetitive four-and-a-half-minute closing vocal hook section that
you could take, despite the meaty celli vying for attention. The 'Hey Jude' and
'Bennie and the Jets' horses had already bolted. Plus 'Bite Your Lip' wasn't
even really disco, which was the big thing then, so it wasn't overly hip with the
kids either. Even in 1976, 'Bite Your Lip' sounded tired. Even drummer Roger
Pope's exciting fast groove couldn't save it – that had already satiated us on the
infinitesimally superior 'One Horse Town' and 'Crazy Water' anyway.

There must have been some hope for the single though, as in the UK it was
a split double A-side with Kiki Dee's 'Chicago', which suggested Elton wanted
to share in the single's potential success much as he'd done by recording her
'Sugar On the Floor' for the 'Island Girl' B-side. But 'Bite Your Lip' did get
radio exposure which helped it reach number 28 on both the UK and USA
singles charts, which is probably enough for me to stifle any further sneezing.

Contemporary Tracks:
'Don't Go Breaking My Heart' (Elton John, Bernie Taupin)

Released as a single A-side, 21 June 1976 (UK and US), b/w 'Snow Queen'. UK: 1.
US: 1. CAN: 1. AUS: 1. NZ: 1.

The first Rocket Records release to feature Elton John as a primary artist
was this infamous duet with Rocket label artist Kiki Dee, issued four months
before the first *Blue Moves* single. Coming up with the title while in the studio
messing around on an electric piano, Elton called Bernie then and there,
asking him to write a duet with that title.

The final lyric could have been twisted to work as a non-duet quite easily,
and the basic track was indeed recorded at the *Blue Moves* sessions, but Elton
decided the song wouldn't work for the album, planning a separate single
instead. Initially, British pop icon Dusty Springfield was approached to sing
on the duet, but she turned it down, it later becoming clear that she had some
kind of throat condition at the time.

On percussionist Ray Cooper's recommendation, keyboardist James
Newton-Howard was given this first opportunity to arrange strings for Elton.
Information is scant on exactly which string section of the three on *Blue Moves*
was used, but I'd guess the full forces of the London Symphony Orchestra
were not required for the duet, and musician's union rules may or may not
have scuppered the possibility of part of the LSO breaking off into a smaller
group anyway. That left the possibility of having used the Gene Page Strings

at Sunset Sound in Los Angeles the same day they played on 'Bite Your Lip', or the Martyn Ford Orchestra back at Abbey Road in London when they did 'One Horse Town' and 'Crazy Water'. My guess is the latter. We do know the duet strings recording occurred prior to Newton-Howard leading the LSO on 'Tonight'. I doubt it was on the same day, but it could have been.

The lack of this one piece of info was bugging me, so to help reach a conclusion, a little audio science was necessary. I listened to all concerned tracks in normal stereo and also with the centre channel removed, which always brings out previously unnoticed instrumental details. The 'Bite Your Lip' Sunset Sound strings sounded like they were in a small-ish space, compared to the duet strings which shared the same richness heard on the Abbey Road songs, indicating a bigger room. Of course, effect units could have been used on the mixes to alter perceived room sizes, but one thing's for sure; you can make a naturally small room sound bigger with an effect, but you'll be working hard to make a recorded large room sound smaller, certainly with the technology that was available in 1976. So, if the duet strings were done at Abbey Road studio 2, any attempt to disguise that room's natural acoustic response would have been futile. Therefore, I conclude that on 'Don't Go Breaking My Heart' we are hearing The Martyn Ford Orchestra at Abbey Road. If anyone can correct me on this, I'd love to hear from you.

The song was arranged in a pastiche style of the Tamla Motown soul duets by Marvin Gaye and Tammi Terrell such as 'Tears at the End of a Love Affair' and 'Ain't Nothing Like the Real Thing'. Upon publishing registration, 'Don't Go Breaking My Heart' was credited to the John/Taupin non-de-plume Ann Orson and Carte Blanche, as was the case with the original registration of 'Hard Luck Story'.

As we know, the song was a monster hit reaching number one not only in the USA, UK, Canada, Australia and New Zealand, but also France, Ireland, South Africa and even Zimbabwe. It was also, quite incredibly, Elton's first number one single at home in the UK. This would not happen for him again until 'Sacrifice' hit the top there in 1990.

'Snow Queen' (Elton John, Bernie Taupin, Kiki Dee, Davey Johnstone, David Nutter)
Released as a single B-side, 21 June 1976 (UK and US), b/w 'Don't Go Breaking My Heart'.
In the pre-compact disc era, vinyl single B-sides were a collective treasure trove. But record makers viewed them as disposable – the A-side was the main concern and the B was a mere side of plastic that had to be filled with anything. But the beauty was that B-sides reaped equivalent royalties to A-sides, that's why the still virtually unknown Kiki Dee song 'Sugar on the Floor' was technically an equal success to its hit A-side, 'Island Girl'.

Within the grooves of these flipsides, you never knew what you'd get, and wonders often awaited. Many of the songs could be referred to as rough diamonds for a variety of reasons. Often, they were undervalued compositions dashed off very quickly. Some were album cuts, which were the most economical way to go because it didn't require any additional recording, plus that way you could still keep the quality up if you cared to.

But sometimes the songs themselves were superlative, even if recorded fast. This was the case with the B-side of 'Don't Go Breaking My Heart', 'Snow Queen'. Credited as another Elton/Kiki duet, it effectively was just another Elton track with Kiki throwing in a chorus harmony and the occasional improvisation.

You can tell it was more or less a one-take situation through the minimalist approach of drums, bass and two acoustic guitars with no overdubs whatsoever. The song was certainly worthy of further attention, but its pecking-order position probably ruled it out. Beneath that simple surface lurked a fine composition. Clearly, care was taken on the musical side as Kiki Dee, Davey Johnstone and rock photographer David Nutter all contributed, giving the song five writers in all. That would have narrowed the royalty split, but, being on the flipside of a huge hit like the A-side here, it didn't matter much.

I'd regard 'Snow Queen's lyric as one of Bernie's finest of the period, thanks to a visual clarity that all but tells you who the subject of the song is. Elton realised as he was singing it that the star of the show was obviously Cher – not just Cher the warm and emphatic entertainer, but apparently a Cher living in her ivory tower.

Arms are spread like icicles upon a frosted cake
The snow queen reigns in a warm L.A.
Behind the cold black gates

But how about proving that passion means more than
A wardrobe of gowns, TV ratings
A fragile waist and a name

Elton described the lyric as 'cutting' and was probably reminded of being invited to perform on Cher's February 1975 TV special where the two had sung 'Bennie and the Jets' together. Mortified, he apologised to her in advance of 'Snow Queen's release, but ever the consummate trooper, Cher had no problem with the faux pas.

'The Goaldiggers Song' (Elton John)
Released as a single A-side, April 1977 (UK), b/w 'Jimmy, Brian, Elton, Eric'.
Only 500 copies were pressed of this Rocket Records UK single for the Goaldiggers soccer charity, used as a promotional device to raise funds for playing fields. Just piano and Elton's double-tracked vocal, the recording was also one of the few examples of him writing a lyric alone, and it wasn't too bad either. He was clearly more capable of this than we'd been led to believe.

'Jimmy, Brian, Elton, Eric'

Released as a single B-side, April 1977 (UK), b/w 'The Goaldiggers Song'.

The B-side of 'The Goaldiggers Song' has almost seven minutes of footballers Jimmy Hill and Brian Moore sitting around talking with Elton and comedian Eric Morecambe about the charity's activities. It has its funny moments. Copies of this rare disc would be quite valuable now.

A Single Man (1978)

Personnel:
Elton John: vocals, piano, clavinet, harmonium, church organ, Mellotron, synthesizer
Herbie Flowers: acoustic bass
Paul Buckmaster: ARP synthesizer
Vicky Brown, Elton John, Davey Johnstone, Stevie Lange, Gary Osborne, Joanne Stone, Chris Thompson, Watford Football Team and The South Audley Street Girls' Choir: backing vocals
Clive Franks: bass
Steve Holley: drums, motor horn
Davey Johnstone, Tim Renwick: guitars, mandolin
B.J. Cole: pedal steel
Ray Cooper: percussion, marimba, vibes
John Crocker: tenor saxophone, clarinet
Jim Shepherd: trombone
Pat Halcox, Henry Lowther: trumpet
Recorded: Jan.-Sept. 1978 at The Mill at Cookham, Berkshire.
Producer: Clive Franks, Elton John
Engineers: Phil Dunne, Stuart Epps, Clive Franks
Arranger: Paul Buckmaster
Release date: 16 October 1978 (UK), 16 October 1978 (US)
Chart placings: UK: 8, US: 15, CAN: 12, AUS: 8 NZ:5

Living in London as a virtual recluse in 1977, Elton only popped his head up for a handful of duo concerts with percussionist Ray Cooper at London's Rainbow Theatre and one or two miscellaneous appearances. In October he recorded some songs in America for a potential album composed and produced by American R&B producer Thom Bell, but the album was shelved with only a three-song EP and two singles being issued in 1979. Then at a concert on 3 November at Wembley Empire Pool where he was accompanied by the band China, Elton announced that he would no longer be touring with a band.

By early 1978, he became enthusiastic to record again after what had ostensibly been a two-year break. Armed with his live sound engineer Clive Franks as producer and bassist, recording began at Gus Dudgeon's private studio, The Mill at Cookham, Berkshire. Gus had bought the property in 1975 with a view to building a studio to remix all of Elton's albums to quadraphonic.

Recording commenced with 'Ego', a Bernie song that had been lying around since the *Blue Moves* days. London session drummer Steve Holley was brought in along with guitarist Tim Renwick. 'Ego' was swiftly issued as a stand-alone single in March 1978, work on the album then continuing.

Ray Cooper was retained for *A Single Man* and guitarist Davey Johnstone made an appearance playing lead on the first single, 'Part-Time Love'. Paul

Buckmaster's arranging skills were utilised for six songs and additionally his synth-playing on the brief instrumental 'Reverie', signalling his last appearance on an Elton album until 1995's .

The major change this time was the absence of Bernie Taupin's contribution. Despite the rumour mill, the separation was a temporary thing caused by the practicalities of he and Elton living in separate countries, coupled with Bernie being busy writing for the new Alice Cooper album, *From the Inside*. Nevertheless, the lyrics on *A Single Man* coincidentally had their fair share of infidelity and breakup themes.

Since the birth of 'Ego' in 1976, Elton's writing had virtually ceased. But in the process of recording that song, new melodies had started flowing. Lyricist Gary Osborne was around, fresh from writing the words for Jeff Wayne's Musical Version of *The War of the Worlds*. Gary and Elton unexpectedly began collaborating on the new music, so it was the old switcharoo for Elton with music now appearing in advance of words. The pair worked together easily. If Elton came up with part of a lyric he wanted to keep, Osborne was happy to accommodate and work around it.

Having an emotional investment in the new work, not helped by the media perceiving it as a comeback, Elton claimed to be nervous as hell about the album. But success wasn't far away with America certifying *A Single Man* as gold in September 1978 and platinum in November. Additionally, 'Part-Time Love' became a respectable top twenty hit. But the single release patterns were convoluted due to MCA baulking at Elton's wish to issue the instrumental 'Song for Guy' as the lead single in America.

Further distinguishing *A Single Man* was the fact it was Elton's first official release in Russia, a positive outcome resulting from he and Ray Cooper playing there as a duo in 1979.

Upon the initial 1978 album release outside the Iron Curtain and having no desire whatsoever to tour with a band, Elton jumped on the talk show treadmill to an extent, talking the record up as far south as Australia. This fuelled further media rumours, this time that he was promoting a conscious image change by dropping the glasses. The simple truth was that upon taking up scuba diving, he realised he was as blind as a bat in the water, then switched to contact lenses. As usual, the media were more interested in the extraneous stuff, but Elton took it in his stride. He was testing the water in more ways than one.

In the context of 1978, *A Single Man* did come across as conventional – even Elton's weirdest music was starting to sound conventional by the current standards – but despite certain weaknesses, the new material contained plenty of substance in songs like the prophetic 'Madness' and the fine 'Shooting Star'.

'Shine on Through' (Elton John, Gary Osborne)

The unwritten law in the audio world is that a song's second recording by the same artist will usually always lack the initial spontaneity and fire captured in the initial fleshed-out demo. There are always exceptions of course and 'Shine on Through' was definitely one of them.

This ballad, seemingly extracted from the 'Sorry Seems to Be the Hardest Word' vein, was originally cut in October 1977 for the shelved Thom Bell-produced album. In stark contrast to that first version, the re-recording that opened *A Single Man* gave the song an opportunity to breathe. It was taken in the classic Elton ballad style and given an arrangement that was more understated than usual. Even Paul Buckmaster's orchestral score was conventional, and the song was better off for that soft approach.

It was a strong, if mellow, lift-off, and was surprising as an album opener, but the current crop of up-tempo tracks lacked clout, and their lyrics were on the darker side. The prior single 'Ego' had been adventurous, experimenting with exotic subject matter, and we can presume that had it been a hit, its manic vitality might have been a contender here for the frontline starting gun.

'Return to Paradise' (Elton John, Gary Osborne)

Released as a single A-side, 3 November 1978 (NZ), b/w 'Song for Guy'.
Released as a single A-side, 17 March 1979 (NET), b/w 'Big Dipper'. NET: 49.

Four or five years earlier, 'Return to Paradise' could have been a hit, at least in Britain. It bore all the hallmarks of a potential MOR chartbuster. Its island rhythm and instrumentation perfectly supported its regret with leaving the sunshine and returning home to the rain. It was also the only track where all instrumentation was arranged by Paul Buckmaster, as he used to do on some early Elton numbers like 'No Shoestrings on Louise'. His arrangement for 'Return to Paradise' certainly gave it an airy and accessible atmosphere.

But a new generation of hit makers and record buyers were coming in underneath, wielding the post-punk banner and stomping all over anything that stunk of adult-contemporary. In the UK, top twenty climbers like The Boomtown Rats, Buzzcocks and Sham 69 were having a damn good stab at sounding the death knell for crowd-pleasing acts like Boney M and hits from clean teen movies like *Grease* - not to mention Elton's mellow instrumental, 'Song for Guy'.

'Return to Paradise' was relegated to the B-side of 'Song for Guy' in Europe but was honoured with A-side status in the Netherlands. Also an A-side in New Zealand, it was completely ignored in favour of the B-side, 'Song for Guy', which was ubiquitous there for the duration of 1979.

'I Don't Care' (Elton John, Gary Osborne)

The return of the urgent Paul Buckmaster string accents is the ingredient that endures on this spry semi-disco dance number. The strings shuffling from urgent low grinds and creamy slides to pure Philadelphia soul on the choruses are an interesting contrast against the flanged verse guitar moves which are difficult to identify as such immediately. Not overdone by any stretch, the production is still inadequate to hide the song's irrelevancy in comparison to those surrounding it.

Scottish pop singer Lulu was attracted to the song enough to cover it in an even more frantic version on her 1979 album, *Don't Take Love for Granted*, giving 'I Don't Care' a slice of extra life.

'Big Dipper' (Elton John, Gary Osborne)
Released as a single B-side, 17 March 1979 (NET), b/w 'Return to Paradise'.

This comical New Orleans-style dirge celebrating specific sexual ideals had a liberal outlook that was ahead of its time. The language was light, but the message was clear. The performances, featuring a section of trumpet, trombone and clarinet, were outstanding. Even the makeshift choir made up of Rocket Records' female staff and the Watford football team sounded like they knew exactly what they were doing.

The final verse lyric, adapted from the Gus Kahn and Walter Donaldson standard 'Makin' Whoopie', helped emphasise the intended novel approach. But this didn't stop 'Big Dipper' (And 'Part-Time Love') being omitted from the 1980 Russian edition of *A Single Man* (Re-titled *Poyot Elton John*) on the grounds of suggestive subject matter. The two songs were not replaced, so the Russian edition possibly had a superior sound considering the potential for wider groove spacing, if indeed a re-mastering even took place to account for that.

'It Ain't Gonna Be Easy' (Elton John, Gary Osborne)
The eight minutes and 23 seconds of side one's slow, bluesy and dynamic closer gave what was essentially Elton's comeback album a taste of a bygone era. The minor-key intro and verse piano chords were evocative of those in *Elton John*'s 'Sixty Years On', but were more literally as rendered by the piano on the emphatic live *17-11-70* version of that song. Plus, you could almost swear the string entry into the second bridge here was leading to the 'Caesar's had your troubles' section from 'The King Must Die'. This all gave 'It Ain't Gonna Be Easy' the semi-unsettling air of Elton's self-titled 1970 breakthrough album but underpinned by a slow funk more reminiscent of *Honky Chateau*'s 'Mellow'.

Under the metaphorical magnifying glass, Buckmaster's orchestral arrangement really came to the party, unobtrusive at first, but finding a lot more to say from the third verse onwards. There it opened out into a smoother, more lush accompaniment to commence the closing play-out section. Angular cello lines then made their appearance, weaving around Ray Cooper's sustained vibes and Elton's striking jazz piano clusters, slowly fading out over the repeating chord sequence covering the entire final three minutes.

This all made this substantial track a hard act to follow. As reflected in the now-famous cliché that was about to enter the rock and roll parlance thanks to Neil Young; 'It's better to burn out than to fade away'. 'It Ain't Gonna Be Easy' provided side one with an opportunity to do both.

'Part-Time Love' (Elton John, Gary Osborne)
Released as a single A-side, 4 October 1978 (UK), November 1979 (US) b/w 'I Cry at Night'. UK: 15. US: 22. CAN: 13. AUS: 12. NZ: 14.

The album's first single, with the exception of the USA where it was not issued until November 1979, this pop song with the guilty spring in its step first hit the UK stores and airwaves in October 1978, two weeks in advance of the album. It was touted by some as Elton's comeback single. It seemed everyone had forgotten the hit and unfortunate miss of the far more imaginative 'Ego' just seven months prior, but expectations were high this time, what with an album accompanying the single.

'Part Time Love' was unique in that it featured Davey Johnstone's last appearance on an Elton record until 1983. Also, due to apparent suggestive subject matter, the song, along with 'Big Dipper', was omitted from the Russian edition of *A Single Man* issued in 1980, giving an eventual tiny piece of inconsequential press to a comeback single by then eclipsed in most places by its successor, 'Song for Guy'. But 'Part Time Love' was no slouch, reaching multiple Top 20 charts and creeping as high as number six in South Africa.

'Georgia' (Elton John, Gary Osborne)
With a gospel piano introduction recalling the work of American singer/songwriter, Randy Newman, 'Georgia' revealed itself to be a potential classic. It's surprising that it didn't attract cover versions in the wake of its release. The chorus was a classic sing-along, as evidenced once again by the dulcet tones of the Watford football team and makeshift South Audley Street Girls' Choir.

Listening today, this ode to the southern state travels along unassumingly, warmed by B.J. Cole's moving pedal steel swells. Then suddenly, out of nowhere in the middle of the final chorus comes the unexpected squelch of a backwards guitar fragment, giving the potential gospel standard a passing moment of psychedelia. It's not incongruous or even obvious, but it's definitely there. The track was an odd surprise on an album that didn't really offer up that many. Indeed, it is a humble album that, like this song, didn't make too big a deal of itself.

'Shooting Star' (Elton John, Gary Osborne)
Similar to 'Georgia', this haunting ballad had 'potential standard' written all over it. Flowing from the same jazz vein as 'Come Down in Time' and 'Idol', 'Shooting Star' demonstrated a stronger and more natural command of the genre, acting as a kind of pivot for Elton's full flowering in the jazz ballad field on the 1982 hit, 'Blue Eyes'.

There is something of the tragic in Gary Osborne's 'Shooting Star' lyric with its lovelorn narrator spellbound in the audience, confronted with the reality of losing the object of their affection to stardom. But on listening, John Crocker's tenor saxophone lines offer some consolation in the face of the hopelessness which the narrator refuses to accept as permanent. It's a theatrical concept not unlike something Taupin could have written for *Goodbye Yellow Brick Road*.

Like Osborne, fresh from contributing to *Jeff Wayne's Musical Version of the War of the Worlds*, acoustic bassist Herbie Flowers was reanimated here for the first time on an Elton album since appearing on 1971's *Madman Across the Water*. His contribution, in conjunction with the Fender Rhodes electric piano, gave the song its smoky alluring quality.

Appearing on what in hindsight was a crucial album in the timeline, 'Shooting Star' was certainly its most sparkling moment and offered up indisputable evidence that Elton John was not done yet.

'Madness' (Elton John, Gary Osborne)

In 'Madness', lyricist Gary Osborne could have been mistaken for having trouble shaking off themes he'd utilised in the *War of the Worlds* lyrics. Either that or in this dramatic lyric about the planting of a bomb, he was having a moment of prophetic clarity concerning situations that have become all too familiar in the 21st Century. Despite those possibilities, the below ten lines must surely be the darkest Elton ever committed to tape.

> *The roar of fire rings out on high*
> *And flames light up the black night sky*
> *A child screams out in fear*
> *A hopeless cry for help*
> *But no one is near enough to hear*
>
> *As walls collapse and timbers flare*
> *The smell of death hangs in the air*
> *When help at last arrives*
> *They try to fight the flames*
> *But nothing survives of all those lives*

Gary Osborne here had the focus and clarity of a pop lyricist with no desire to mince his words. The contrast between that and Bernie Taupin's often abstract metaphors was palpable. Elton did nothing by half-measures, and if the decision to change to another lyricist had to be made, this new recipe was a successful outcome.

The only true rock song on the album, the style supported the lyrical concept perfectly, with the added drama of Paul Buckmaster's orchestral arrangement. But the strings were unobtrusive, sticking to the occasional disco-style interjection and leaving the tension to reside in the chords themselves, which were intense enough whatever instruments were uttering them.

Australia's Countdown TV show host, Molly Meldrum, clearly saw the dark beauty in 'Madness', inviting Elton to perform the song (mimed) on the episode of Sunday 10 December 1978.

'Reverie' (Elton John)

This brief piano turnaround of less than a minute, consisting of two sections with synthesizer melody played by Paul Buckmaster, was not without its charms. The tiny instrumental was more complex than, and acted as an introduction for, 'Song for Guy'.

'Song for Guy' (Elton John)

Released as a single A-side, 28 November 1978 (UK), March 1979 (US) b/w 'Lovesick'. UK: 4. US: 110. AUS: 14.
Released as a single B-side, 3 November 1978 (NZ), b/w 'Return to Paradise'. NZ: 7.
In a December 1978 interview on Australia's Countdown TV show, Elton described 'Song for Guy' as an optimistic death song. When asked in contemporary interviews how he came up with the instrumental, he would sometimes begin the story with the quip, 'I wrote it on a Sunday, and my heart stood still, Da doo ron ron ron, Da doo ron ron.'

He was messing with interviewers just like he was messing around with some piano chords one Sunday imagining the soul leaving the body at the point of death. Producer Clive Franks hauled out the Roland Rhythm Box and the piece was recorded on the spot. Elton multi-tracked acoustic piano in separate octaves, adding Mellotron, Polymoog and Solina string synthesizer. Franks played bass, and later Ray Cooper layered shaker and wind chimes on top - one repeated line of lyric courtesy of Elton, 'Life isn't everything', and it was done.

Seventeen-year-old Guy Burchett was the messenger boy at Rocket Records. Sadly, he died in a motorcycle accident, the common belief being that Elton then wrote the piece as a tribute. The truth was a little stranger. The song was composed and recorded before Elton knew about the accident. In fact, the recording and the accident took place on the same Sunday, quite possibly simultaneously. Elton was wondering what to call the piece. Given the tragic news the following day, the dedication was natural.

Released as the album's second UK single in November 1978, it enjoyed success there peaking at number four, also reaching seven in New Zealand where it was ubiquitous throughout 1979.

Not charting at all in Canada, the situation for the single in the USA was complex. Elton wanted the track to be the first single in America. MCA Records baulked at this, claiming an instrumental could not be a hit. But Elton got his way, the single being issued there in March 1979. In response, MCA followed up with little promotion. As a result, the single barely charted, though it did reach 37 on the Adult Contemporary chart. The entire debacle instigated Elton's decision to move to Geffen Records in 1981, the song, therefore, being reflective of more than one ending.

Contemporary Tracks:
'Ego' (Elton John, Bernie Taupin)
Released as a single A-side, 21 March 1978 (UK), March 1978 (US) b/w 'Flintstone

Boy'. UK: 34. US: 34. CAN: 21. AUS: 40.

The whole so-called comeback thing had really been kicked into gear back on 21 March 1978 by the release of this spirited and idiosyncratic single. The song had been lying around unrecorded for two years, so it was the first thing tackled when Elton dove back into the studio waters. The recording was a fast-moving and dramatic piece of audio theatre reflecting the unpleasant underbelly of rock and roll. Elton had high hopes for the single, and an expensive video was made to accompany it.

But in 1978 he was amongst a coterie of targets some of the music press were giving less than positive coverage. The others were mainly progressive rockers, like Yes and Genesis, but a fair amount of what critics considered as soft rock artists were included. Of course, by now punk had blown the doors off, wanting something or anything to happen to instigate change.

As a rabid music consumer, Elton was quite open about his love for the new post-punk vanguard as it had delivered substantial artists like Elvis Costello, Ian Dury and edgy units like Buzzcocks. So, the 'Ego' single's lack of success was disappointing in light of the clear sonic tribute it made to the new musical movement. In fact, 'Ego' was a very early example of synthesizer-driven new wave pop and sounded like nothing else that was on the British charts at the time. With Kate Bush's adventurous and perplexing 'Wuthering Heights' being number one in the UK the week 'Ego' came out, you'd presume the single-buying public might have embraced something almost equally as audacious that they could also dance to.

'Ego' was the closest thing to new wave that Elton ever released and it did make the Top 40 in the UK, USA and Australia, being most successful hitting 21 in Canada. But it wasn't enough, and Elton was disappointed. We can only imagine the more confident and adventurous musical direction *A Single Man* might have taken had it had 'Ego' as a worldwide hit to bolster its creation.

'Flintstone Boy' (Elton John)

Released as a single B-side, 21 March 1978 (UK), March 1978 (US) b/w 'Ego'.

At face value, the B-side 'Flintstone Boy' came across as a throwaway. The name Flintstone immediately gave it a comical stigma which didn't help either. Not to be taken seriously maybe, but I doubt it was intended to be serious.

Listening today, there's a lot here to like. For a start, it's unique in being the only fully Elton-written lyric released since the 'I've Been Loving You'/'Here's to the Next Time' single in 1968. Plus, the song has more than enough strong and memorable hooks for a respectable A-side, the least of which isn't the seemingly overt 'Walk on the Wild Side' bass quote that occurs twice in the final verse. That's a tasteful touch.

It's as if this recording had the benefit of having enough time available to get the best result out of it, even though it's unlikely it was anywhere near the top of the list. Not that it would have taken very long to record if the band played together and the second guitar overdub was added later. Maybe the synthesizer was an overdub too. There were also the vocal harmonies to add. I'd say the track was recorded in half an hour to an hour tops. They could have easily been a lot more slapdash with this recording, but no, however easy it might have been to get done, care was taken. And it showed.

'I Cry at Night' (Elton John, Bernie Taupin)

Released as a single B-side, 4 October 1978 (UK), November 1979 (US) b/w 'Part Time Love'.

This finely-wrought Taupin lyric was written around the time of recording the *Blue Moves* album. Considered to be referring to the breakdown of Bernie's marriage, 'I Cry at Night' is absolutely believable as such with the narrator's claim that the house he lives in has no reason and he's been 'Ten years a slave to rock and roll'. But most telling is the evidence in the imagery.

The sun once shone through the tire swing
The dogs barked and bayed in the winter and spring
And the ivy that hung now sadly clings to a dying season

For the yellow grass on the sun-burnt lawn
Sleeps in her seed from the sunset to dawn
And just like your love that's come and gone
It goes on breathing

Those lyrics are certainly a good argument for the common belief that personal misery spawns great art. It's not necessarily true as a rule, but it definitely worked in this case, if the above marriage-breakup inspiration theory is true. Bernie could just as easily have been euphoric when he wrote this, which I could also believe. Artistic output is not necessarily reflective of the emotional state at the time of writing, but it *can* be, and Elton's stark, solo, and at times angry performance here is a further clue that leaves little to the imagination, at least in regard to the narrator's mindset.

Perhaps considered a bit dark in tone for inclusion on *A Single Man*, this new addition to the treasure trove of Elton John B-sides found a home on the flipside of 'Part Time Love'. I bought this single when I was eleven, so whether the lyrics came from a specific life experience or not, it was obvious to me even then that this track meant heavy business.

'Lovesick' (Elton John, Bernie Taupin)

Released as a single B-side, 28 November 1978 (UK), March 1979 (US) b/w 'Song for Guy'.

This disco/Philadelphia soul hybrid was a complete stylistic contrast to its A-side, the soft instrumental, 'Song for Guy'. The brisk whiteness of 'Lovesick' placed it just on the wrong side of both genres in a kind of no-mans-land of safe harmless dancing, undisturbed by any danger of rhythmic feel or funk syncopation. It also sounded as if it was taken a bit fast just to get it out of the way. Happily, it was redeemed by the icing of a quality string arrangement, at first conventional but becoming more pointed, angular and interesting as the song faded out. But the cherry on top was a committed guitar solo from Tim Renwick sounding every bit as noble as his electric solo on Al Stewart's 1976 hit, 'Year of the Cat'.

'Strangers' (Elton John, Gary Osborne)

Released as a single B-side, 14 September 1979 (UK and US), b/w 'Victim of Love'. The 1978 *A Single Man* sessions yielded this slow shuffle ballad. After the 'Mama Can't Buy You Love' single was successful in the USA, 'Strangers' was planned as its UK B-side, pressed for August 1979 release, but cancelled at the last minute in favour of 'Victim of Love' as the A-side. This was presumably to work with the *Victim of Love* album release scheduled for October.

The lyric by Gary Osborne could easily be mistaken as the work of Bernie, metaphorically reflecting two people in a high-wire act with a watching audience wondering if they'll make it across. The two have made the 'long and lonely climb', only to find they were 'strangers from the start'. Perhaps the concept sprung from Elton as was the case with some of the John/Osborne songs.

Ex-Eagles member Randy Meisner released 'Strangers' as a single from his self-titled 1982 album. Stunted and out of step with the times, the semi-duet with Heart's Ann Wilson was nevertheless stronger for its dramatic orchestral arrangement courtesy of Paul Buckmaster.

Are You Ready for Love (UK EP) / Mama Can't Buy You Love (US EP) (1979)

Personnel:
Elton John: vocals
LeRoy Bell, Tony Bell, Carla Benson, Evette Benton, Barbara Ingram, Casey James, Bill Lamb, The Spinners: backing vocals
Bob Babbit: bass
Charles Collins: drums
Leroy M. Bell, Tony Bell, Bobby Eli, Casey James: guitars
Thom Bell, Casey James: keyboards
Larry Washington: percussion
M.F.S.B: strings & horns
Recorded: October 1977 at Kay Smith Studio, Seattle, Washington and Sigma Sound Studios, Philadelphia, Pennsylvania.
Producer: Peter Bellotte
Engineers: Don Murray, Buzz Richmond, Jeff Stewart
Release date: 30 April 1979 (UK), June 1979 (US)
Chart placings: UK: 42 (1979 'Are You Ready For Love' 7"), US: 9 ('Mama Can't Buy You Love' 7"), CAN: 10 ('Mama Can't Buy You Love' 7"), AUS: 63 ('Are You Ready For Love' 7"), 82 ('Mama Can't Buy You Love' 7"), NZ: 20 ('Mama Can't Buy You Love' 7")

'Philadelphia Freedom' had shown Elton's love for Philadelphia soul. Moving more in that direction and choosing to not contribute to the songwriting, he cut some tracks in October 1977 with legendary Philadelphia soul producer, Thom Bell, who'd earned his reputation through multiple hits by The Delfonics and The Stylistics.

Recording took place at Kay Smith Studio in Seattle, Thom Bell's then-current home, and in Philadelphia at Sigma Sound, the home of Philadelphia soul. Musicians were from the M.F.S.B collective, a large group of session players based out of Sigma Sound. But the relationship between Elton and Bell broke down to an extent before an album could be completed, possibly due to Bell indicating that Elton sung too high, was not using his voice correctly and didn't use his lower register enough.

This three-track EP was culled from the recordings, mixed by Elton and Clive Franks in January 1979 at London's Utopia Studios and issued in the UK in April. 'Are You Ready for Love' was the lead track, the full-length version of which took up side one of the EP, backed with 'Three Way Love Affair' and 'Mama Can't Buy You Love'.

The American 12" issued in June 1979 was titled *Mama Can't Buy You Love* and featured that song in the prime A-side position with the other two on the B-side. 'Are You Ready for Love' was not issued as a 7" single in the USA.

In February 1989, MCA issued The Complete Thom Bell Sessions which consisted of Bell's original 1977 mixes, the most striking difference being verse two of 'Are You Ready for Love' which featured lead vocals by John Edwards and Bobby Smith of American R&B group The Spinners.

'Are You Ready for Love' (LeRoy Bell, Thom Bell, Casey James)
Released as a 7" single A-side, 30 April 1979 (UK), b/w 'Are You Ready for Love Pt. II'. UK: 42. AUS: 63. DEN: 13.
Released as a 7" single A-side, 31 May 1979 (US), b/w 'Three Way Love Affair'.
Issued simultaneously with the EP in the UK was a 7" which split 'Are You Ready for Love' into Part I and II over both sides of the single, in the presentation style of many soul and disco singles of the period. Co-writers on the song were Thom Bell's nephew LeRoy Bell and Casey James of Philadelphia soul group, Bell and James.

The song may have been the most positive track of the three, but it was also the least interesting. Its highest chart position was number thirteen in Denmark. On a further positive note, an edit of Elton and Clive's 1979 remix was a surprise UK number one in 2003.

'Three Way Love Affair' (LeRoy Bell, Casey James)
Released as a 7" single B-side, June 1979 (US), July 1979 (AUS and NZ), b/w 'Mama Can't Buy You Love'.
The carefree rhythmic bounce of 'Three Way Love Affair' defied its dark reflection of a deteriorating relationship. Elton sounded as happy as a clam on it, and certainly looked that way in the promotional footage of him singing (or most likely miming) it in the studio, despite enduring an interminable amount of end choruses that went beyond the bounds of the single length. The musicianship was superlative, as to be expected from the pool of M.F.S.B musicians. 'Three Way Love Affair' was pretty slick and virtually of A-side quality.

'Mama Can't Buy You Love' (LeRoy Bell, Casey James)
Released as a 7" single A-side, June 1979 (US), July 1979 (AUS and NZ), b/w 'Mama Can't Buy You Love'. US: 9 and 1 (AC). CAN: 10. AUS: 82. NZ: 20.
In 1979 this rhythmically happy-go-lucky shuffle was the most successful cull from the Thom Bell sessions. The 7" single hit number 9 in the USA, but was number 1 Adult Contemporary and 36 R&B. After the single's success in America, it was pressed in the UK with 'Strangers' on the flipside. But the release was pulled at the last minute in favour of an A-side of 'Victim of Love', which made sense with that song's namesake album release waiting in the wings.

The Complete Thom Bell Sessions was issued in 1989 consisting of Thom Bell's original 1977 mixes. His mix of 'Mama Can't Buy You Love' was smoother, with the string section more to the foreground. The 1979 single, of course, was Elton and Clive Franks' more detailed remix which focused more on rhythmic drum intricacies, assets which were all but inaudible on Thom Bell's original mix.

Contemporary Tracks:
'Nice and Slow' (Elton John, Bernie Taupin, Thom Bell)
Released on an album, *The Complete Thom Bell Sessions*, February 1989.
Released as a single B-side, November 2004, b/w 'All That I'm Allowed (I'm Thankful)'.

Objectively, this sex-appreciation lyric worked fine. But subjectively, lyrically and musically it embodied all that so many would disparage the coming *Victim of Love* songs for, in the process outdoing every single one of those songs tenfold, and not in a good way. If this Thom Bell session outtake had been available in 1979, it would have made *Victim of Love* sound like the beloved *Sgt Pepper's Lonely Hearts Club Band* and *Dark Side of the Moon* on steroids.

Lulu saw something in the song, recording it along with 'I Don't Care' for her 1979 album, *Don't Take Love for Granted*. Her innocent sounding take gave 'Nice and Slow' a twist that worked. But if the naysayers had been exposed to Elton's version at that time, they surely would have viewed the song as being Elton and Bernie dangerously close to their lowest ebb. Thankfully the 1989 release of the Thom Bell outtakes slipped 'Nice and Slow' into the repertoire without a fuss, even opening the album with it. Bold.

'Country Love Song' (Joseph Jefferson)
Released on an album, *The Complete Thom Bell Sessions*, February 1989.

I'd describe the decision to record this song in the Thom Bell sessions as baffling, to say the least. Written by ex-Manhattans drummer turned soul songwriter Joseph Jefferson, the lyric's first draft ambiguities, unworthy of quote, needed further work. Even 'Nice and Slow' was a superior beast. The instrumental and vocal performances were fine, but thanks to the composition, 'Country Love Song' was and is the number one Elton cut of them all, but at the other end of the spectrum.

'Shine on Through' (Elton John, Gary Osborne)
Released on an album, *The Complete Thom Bell Sessions*, February 1989.

Taken as a ballad with strings in the Philadelphia R&B style producer Thom Bell was known for, you'd think this track would have had more panache. But listening now, there is something cold about the recording. The rhythm track and strings work well, but at well over seven minutes it's lengthy, and minus any guitar licks or instrumental improvisation to spice it up and retain interest along the way. It's kind of like they lost interest without quite finishing it. Or maybe they realised it was the wrong song for the treatment. Unfortunately, 'Shine on Through' was wasted here.

Victim of Love (1979)

Personnel:
Elton John: vocals
Michael McDonald, Patrick Simmons, Stephanie Spruill, Julia Waters, Maxine
Waters: backing vocals
Marcus Miller: bass
Keith Forsey: drums
Tim Cansfield, Steve Lukather, Craig Snyder: guitars
Thor Baldursson, Roy Davies: keyboards
Paulinho Da Costa: percussion
Lenny Pickett: saxophone
Recorded: August 1979 at Musicland, Munich and Rusk Sound Studios, Hollywood.
Producer: Pete Bellotte
Engineers: Peter Luedmann, Hans Menzel, Carolyn Tapp
Arranger: Thor Baldursson
Release date: 13 October 1979 (UK), 13 October 1979 (US)
Chart placings: UK: 41, US: 35, CAN: 28, AUS: 20 NZ: 44

We have arrived at what some might view as the elephant in the room. Why? The salient facts are these. The 1979 album was helmed by Munich Machine disco super-producer Pete Bellotte. He had overseen Donna Summer megahits like 1975's 'Love to Love You Baby', and with electronic pop master Georgio Moroder, Summer's forward-thinking dance-floor mega-thumper 'I Feel Love', followed by her 'Macarthur Park', 'Hot Stuff' and 'Bad Girls' singles. Elton wrote and played nothing on *Victim of Love*, appearing for just one day to sing the songs. Additional overdubs were performed by the crème de la crème of west coast session players at L.A.'s Rusk Sound Studios.

As far as the fans were concerned, the idea of Elton John going disco was a recipe for disaster. As far as the critics were concerned, it was an excuse for denigration. A general lack of objectivity on the subject settled like a mist that blinkered so many as to be incapable of seeing any worth in the album. The fans simply didn't want Elton to change direction or churn out fodder – understandable. Some music critics were blinded by whatever current trends they considered relevant and others by simply refusing to recognise a quality performance within a field they detested. Those critics lumped all disco together, forgetting that within that sobriquet there was both good and bad and it was their job to inform the public on the differences. In this case, they failed.

They may not have been the most crafted songs ever committed to vinyl, but they certainly weren't the worst. The quality of the musicianship was undeniable, not to mention the mixes, which were sonically superb. But in New York's *Village Voice*, critic Robert Christgau described *Victim of Love* as 'Incredibly drab'. In the 13 December, 1979 issue of *Rolling Stone*, music critic Stephen Holden declared, '*Victim of Love* hasn't a breath of life'. This was despite guitarist Steve Lukather's masterful soloing and keyboardist Thor Baldursson's sensational synth-layering on the menacing hook line of 'Thunder in the Night' alone. I thought the reviewer's goal would have been to provide an accurate reflection of what resided within the grooves, and his function to pay attention through a prism of some modicum of musical understanding. With such attention, maybe the clear presence of an emerging and monstrous talent like bass player Marcus Miller, leaving his warm tones and syncopated attacks all over the record, wouldn't have been missed altogether. Had such an expectation of a music critic who also claimed there were 'No interesting instrumental breaks' been satisfied, perhaps Tower of Power saxophonist Lenny Pickett's virtuosic 'Johnny B. Goode' solo and Steve Lukather's precise and gleaming 'Born Bad' guitar solo would have both been diagnosed as exactly what they were – faultless. In the case of Lukather, 'Born Bad' was perhaps the most virtuosic guitar solo committed to an Elton John record yet.

But it wasn't to be.

You'd think with the record-buying public being clearly prepared to accept the Bee Gees' entry into disco to the tune of buying millions of albums and singles, surely Elton John doing something similar shouldn't have been too alienating for them? But the issue was timing. *Saturday Night Fever* had first infected the public system in November 1977, almost a full two years before *Victim of Love,* and the fallout from the movie's endless raft of successful singles was still being felt in late 1979. Those singles were absolutely unavoidable, and the public were naturally growing weary of the disco trend. So too, the music press, if they had anything at all to do with steering the public taste towards anything else. So hugely popular was *Saturday Night Fever* and its soundtrack that they, in fact, struck the death knell for disco. In the wake of all this, *Victim of Love* appeared as a mere blip - too little too late. Had it been early 1978, things might have been different.

Single choices possibly dogged the new album's success too. First single 'Victim of Love' was a downer, and second single 'Johnny B. Goode' might have been a popular standard, but the chances of the disco kids getting on board with its rock and roll vibe were slim. The obvious single, though not the strongest song, was surely 'Spotlight' - a basic song about dancing. With an album of only seven songs and three of them downers at title level, single options were few.

The album was originally to be titled *Thunder in the Night*, after the side two opener, which might have been some improvement and at least been a bit tougher-sounding. But that wasn't to be either. Further compounding things, the songs were all linked together with virtually the same tempo and disco beat, providing little variation from track to track.

Elton made it clear going forward that he didn't regret making the record. It just didn't appear to be what the public wanted, although it did reach a respectable number 20 in Australia. In its favour, the album was at least a definitive and consistent statement – an attribute that music critics always seemed to value so highly, but somehow totally missed in this instance.

Victim of Love was not the last disco record ever made, but it was quite possibly the last great pure disco record made. It put a full stop on the classic disco period, effectively closing the '70s, albeit inviting behind it quite a huge door-slam, trailing a long reverberation.

'Johnny B. Goode' (Chuck Berry)

Released as a 7" and 12" single A-side, December 1979 (UK, AUS and NZ), b/w 'Thunder in the Night'.

Released as a 7" single A-side, December 1979 (US and CAN), b/w 'Georgia'.

Starting a pure disco record with Chuck Berry's guitar intro originally on loan from boogie-woogie great Louis Jordan, was a fun moment of irony that *Victim of Love* offered up before the kick-drum onslaught began.

Berry's 1958 single was an instant hit but, unfortunately, Elton's single didn't chart. The 7" was a 3m:22s edit and the UK 12" single was the full 8m:06s version. But the inclusion of that full-length version on *Victim of Love* demanded a feat of endurance from listeners, to say the least.

On the positive side, New York bassist Marcus Miller, here at the dawn of a powerhouse career, tastefully complimented Keith Forsey's already solid drum foundation by dominating with individual skill and a signature bass tone that was plain to hear - most predominantly in the breakdown at 4m:33s.

Elsewhere, Tower of Power tenor saxophonist Lenny Pickett, in his first appearance on an Elton album since 1974's *Caribou*, demonstrated his ear-shattering range reaching beyond the believable scope of the instrument.

'Johnny B. Goode', backed with 'Thunder in the Night', was Elton's final single release of the 1970s.

'Warm Love in a Cold World' (Peter Bellotte, Gunther Moll, Stefan Wisnet)

Marcus Miller was at the forefront again here, this time responsible for the main guitar hook overdubbed on the bass above his solid lower grounding. The central breakdown section created more interest with striking guitar harmonies courtesy of 21-year-old Steve Lukather, already well-established from a myriad of sessions for artists including Boz Scaggs, Alice Cooper and Barbra Streisand - not to mention newfound success with his own band, Toto.

The album pattern was forming. Despite having three songwriters, 'Warm Love in a Cold World' was lukewarm but supported by hot musicians that were on top of their game. Better that than the other way around.

'Born Bad' (Peter Bellotte, Geoff Bastow)

Released as a 12" single A-side, 1979 (IT), b/w 'Victim of Love'.

Another downer perhaps but 'Born Bad' was an improvement on the prior song. Again, the session players saved the day. The backing vocalists gave some welcome vocal variation before a melodically stunning Steve Lukather guitar solo. It's the kind of thing budding guitarists back in the day would sit around for hours trying to replicate. It's Lukather focusing on the notes themselves with a mostly clean and pointed sound pushing just the right amount of distortion. For these 30 seconds, the fact that you're in disco land is irrelevant, as the solo is the overall high point of the album.

'Thunder in the Night' (Peter Bellotte, Michael Hoffman)
Released as a 7" and 12" single B-side, December 1979 (UK, AUS and NZ), b/w 'Johnny B. Goode'.
Originally considered for the album title itself, 'Thunder in the Night' at least kept its negative content less obvious at lyric level. Listening to the words would have revealed that this nevertheless richly dark and beautifully synth-laden breakup song probably didn't have what it took to climb the chart ladder as a hit single. But in its defence, it was the album's finest composition.

Spotlight' (Peter Bellotte, Gunther Moll, Stefan Wisnet)
Finally, a happier song appeared. For the purposes of general popularity, a basic song about dancing surely had a better shot at being a hit than the darker tracks. This one had several vocal and instrumental hooks to its credit and was obvious single fodder by anyone's standard. But it was overlooked. If released as a single it might have received more of a critical drubbing than the clearly superior composition 'Victim of Love', but surely not more than the time-travelling 'Johnny B. Goode'.

'Street Boogie' (Peter Bellotte, Gunther Moll, Stefan Wisnet)
A possible single choice alternative to 'Spotlight' could have been the slightly grittier 'Street Boogie'. 'Boogie' was a buzzword then, used for everything from song titles to popular hit compilations, like *Don't Walk, Boogie*. This song could have been a contender. Maybe they just didn't want to clutter up the airwaves with even more songs about dancing. Wise move.

'Victim of Love' (Peter Bellotte, Sylvester Levay, Jerry Rix)
Released as a single A-side, 14 September 1979 (UK and US), b/w 'Strangers'. US: 31. CAN: 46. AUS: 38.
The title track and first single was co-written by resident Munich recording artist and composer Sylvester Levay, who co-wrote the international hit 'Fly Robin Fly' for German disco group Silver Convention. 'Victim of Love' also featured Doobie Brothers members Michael McDonald and Patrick Simmons on backing vocals. McDonald was having a run of success, his familiar vocal colour highlighting hits like Steely Dan's 'Peg' and the current Kenny Loggins single, 'This Is It', not to mention McDonald's lead vocals on the two recent Doobie Brothers hits, 'What a Fool Believes' and 'Minute By Minute'. His vocal

presence at least helped give 'Victim of Love' a sound familiar and relevant to current pop radio.

Peaking in the US at number 31, it was probably only the lyric's negative connotation that halted the single in its tracks. It wasn't as blatantly 'discofied' as some of its album companions, and the interminable four-on-the-floor dance beat was given some relief with the occasional syncopated push. But there was no disguising the intended home for the song's 128 beats-per-minute.

Outroduction

The above-examined discography simply wouldn't (or couldn't) have followed quite the same curve had Elton John started out at any other point in time. How did the music develop from psychedelic art song into finding its maturity as a combination of moody orchestral epics and semi-glam rockers? How did Elton's immersion in Bernie Taupin's kaleidoscope of trans-Atlantic myth, fact and confession, morph through success into glossy commercial soul and German production-line disco, pondering little more than heartbreak woes from which Elton sounded emotionally distant? The answer is sort of a cliché – the eclectic musical twists and turns and the freedom to indulge in them were simply a reflection of the times.

In the '60s, songwriters like Bob Dylan and The Beatles proved that you were only limited by your imagination, leading to the bursting of an experimental bubble. By the 1970s, record companies had huge budgets and were willing to invest in artist development, giving new artists years to perfect their work towards projected profit margin outcomes. The public also cared. Music, along with movies, was the primary source of entertainment.

It was all of this that allowed Elton John the freedom to move, to try things. If something didn't work, he'd try something else. If he'd been launched five years later, things could have been very different and such a rotation of successful albums may not have been possible. Even by the late '70s, recording budgets were being tightened up. The certainty of a surefire hit became the goal more than ever before. The privilege of an artist being given years of development to find their feet was slowly diminishing. Elton's extensive '70s discography stood and stands for the most part as a portrait of artistic freedom. Seven globally successful albums, two of them doubles, in five years from 1972 to 1976, was an achievement that for a variety of reasons would become more difficult for anyone to achieve. Even Michael Jackson's core solo success was concentrated into only three albums over a nine-year period before the circle began closing in.

So, Elton's choice to change tack and relinquish composition and instrumental duties to outside producers of commercial genres like disco was, rather than a misguided mistake, a privilege that he and many artists had in that period, and was one that he had certainly earned.

Elton John and Bernie Taupin had what it took and worked themselves into the ground for the achievements of their first decade. But they were also very lucky. If you had talent and wanted to take advantage of any luck the music business might bestow upon you, the 1970s was the time to do it. In that decade, Elton was philosophical about the business, often telling interviewers that pop music was disposable. He made the following quote in a 1974 Rolling Stone interview:

'There are so many people who think they're the big cheese – "Well, man, we played for 70,000 people." Well, it's great, sure, but I mean, who cares?

*Next year someone else will be able to do it. Your next-door neighbour
might do it. And that's the whole point of pop music. That's the fun of it,
the thrill of it.'*

That quote had a refreshing lack of pretentiousness for someone who at the
time virtually had the world at his feet. His late-70s lull may have come about,
and he may have expected it, but it had also occurred for more than a few
other rock stars. Some never recovered their careers. But for Elton and Bernie,
there was hope, if the lyrics from the 1979 B-side, 'Strangers', had anything to
do with it. These Gary Osborne lyrics coincidentally but uncannily reflected the
situation of the Captain and the kid at the close of the '70s.

*Two people caught in the tide
On the edge of love and pride
And both afraid to approach the side
And fall again*

*Two people playing the part
But which is life and which is art
And isn't it a little late
To start it all again*

Fortunately for the fans and everyone else concerned, it wasn't too late. Not
too late at all.

Also from Sonicbond Publishing

On Track series
Queen Andrew Wild 978-1-78952-003-3
Emerson Lake and Palmer Mike Goode 978-1-78952-000-2
Deep Purple and Rainbow 1968-79 Steve Pilkington 978-1-78952-002-6
Yes Stephen Lambe 978-1-78952-001-9
Blue Oyster Cult Jacob Holm-Lupo 978-1-78952-007-1
The Beatles Andrew Wild 978-1-78952-009-5
Roy Wood and the Move James R Turner 978-1-78952-008-8
Genesis Stuart MacFarlane 978-1-78952-005-7
Jethro Tull Jordan Blum 978-1-78952-016-3
The Rolling Stones 1963-80 Steve Pilkington 978-1-78952-017-0
Judas Priest John Tucker 978-1-78952-018-7
Toto Jacob Holm-Lupo 978-1-78952-019-4
Van Der Graaf Generator Dan Coffey 978-1-78952-031-6
Frank Zappa 1966 to 1979 Eric Benac 978-1-78952-033-0
Elton John in the 1970s Peter Kearns 978-1-78952-034-7
The Moody Blues Geoffrey Feakes 978-1-78952-042-2
The Beatles Solo 1969-1980 Andrew Wild 978-1-78952-042-2
Steely Dan Jez Rowden 978-1-78952-043-9

On Screen series
Carry On... Stephen Lambe 978-1-78952-004-0
Audrey Hepburn Ellen Cheshire 978-1-78952-011-8
Powell and Pressburger Sam Proctor 978-1-78952-013-2
Seinfeld Seasons 1 to 5 Stephen Lambe 978-1-78952-012-5
Francis Ford Coppola Stephen Lambe 978-1-78952-022-4

Other Books
Not As Good As The Book Andy Tillison 978-1-78952-021-7
The Voice. Frank Sinatra in the 1940s
Stephen Lambe 978-1-78952-032-3

and many more to come!